EDZ: still on the trail!
Happy Christmas
Roger
1986

Peter Verstappen was born in California and educated in Europe, Colorado and New England. He is a columnist, a consultant to the British Government on tourism and runs an international marketing consultancy. He has been, among other things, a copper miner, president of an advertising agency and a radio announcer. Peter Verstappen has lived in England for thirteen years and has made his home in Richmond, Surrey.

The Book of Surnames

Origins and Oddities of Popular Names

PETER VERSTAPPEN

SPHERE BOOKS LIMITED
30–32 Gray's Inn Road, London WC1X 8JL

First published in Great Britain by
Pelham Books Ltd 1980

Published by Sphere Books Ltd 1982

TRADE
MARK

Printed and bound in Great Britain by
Cox & Wyman Ltd, Reading

TO

Margaret Evans Thomas Kilroy Verstappen

AND

Henri Verstappen,

PROOF POSITIVE THAT SURNAMES COMBINE
WITH IMPROBABLE RESULTS

COMPILED AND EDITED BY:

Peter Verstappen

WRITERS:

Pat Lyons, Paul Strathern, Peter Vestappen

SENIOR RESEARCHERS:

Hilary Whyte, Wendy Verstappen

RESEARCHERS:

Eric Bernhard, Kimberly A. Bowman, Thomas Cussans, Geoffrey Doran, Alan Heathcote, Katherine Thornton, Don Wilson

PROFESSIONAL CONSULTANTS:

John Dodgson, President – English Place Name Society, and Reader – University College, London; and Peter McClure, Reader – University of Hull

CONTROLLER:

Glenn Irvine

SECRETARIAL ASSISTANTS:

Staff of Stevenson & Partners: Stephanie Bell, Tony Edwards, Lorraine Gannon, Janet Haine, Elizabeth Robinson, Jane Stevenson. Also Chris Alton, Sharon Howe, Barbara Jackson, Noel Ruschweyh, Annie Stewart.

CONTENTS

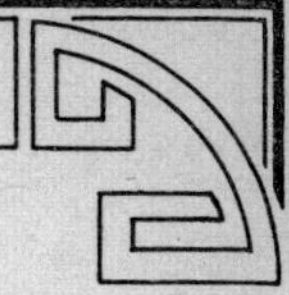

INTRODUCTION

This is a book about Britain's most popular surnames. Just seventy-six surnames account for over fourteen million Britons – one quarter of the entire population. When the 1000-plus surnames which relate directly to these seventy-six names are taken into account, another quarter of the population is included. Thus *The Book of Surnames* has been written with half the population in mind.

Smith is by far our most popular name, as it is in most of the English-speaking world. There are close to one million Smiths in the United Kingdom. Jones, Williams, Brown and Taylor are the runners up. Each has over 400,000 namesakes. However, common surnames are by no means confined to these top five. Even our twentieth most common name, Edwards, has over 200,000 standard bearers.

In the pages which follow, the book sets out to explore the many remarkable aspects of these popular last names.

THE RISE OF SURNAMES

Perhaps surprisingly, surnames are a relatively recent phenomenon. Most experts believe that they came into common use in the eleventh century, so they've yet to be around for a thousand years.

Surnames were needed for a variety of reasons. The growth of cities was certainly one of these. A man could be known as just plain John in a small village but the designation simply wasn't specific enough in a city. So he became 'John the Baker', 'John at the Water', and so on. Three other events helped surnames to spread.

The first, taxes, were hardly new in the year 1000. However, about then they did become better organised and the record-keeping which resulted required an accurate designation of those on the rolls.

Secondly, man was becoming a far more communal animal.

In virtually all cases this coming together involved a contractual, though often unwritten, exchange of loyalties. Families owed their allegiance to and expected protection from others. In turn, others were allied to and protected by them. Over the course of time these relationships became codified and in the process gave rise to a large number of surnames, as we shall see in the chapters which follow.

Finally, as Christianity spread, baptism and (often) subsequent confirmation came to be common.

All the above normally involved written records and, perforce, the ability to designate accurately one person as opposed to another. Thus surnames became an absolute necessity. The story of how our names came about and how they've changed takes up much of each of the chapters in this book.

ROOTS AND FOREIGN BRANCHES

The Book of Surnames examines seventy-six major surnames. It explores their ancestry and lists over one thousand other names which share part or all of the same background. Where a name comes from, how it grew and when it first appeared are all covered. With rare exceptions the precise roots for any given surname are ambiguous this is notably true of the British Isles. Over the centuries Britain has received a vast host of (sometimes unwanted) foreign visitors. So the roots of British surnames have many branches. As a result a Cornishman and a Scot may share a common surname, but for entirely different reasons.

The book does not attempt to identify *all* sources and roots for all the names covered. There are two good reasons for this. Many origins are lost in the mists of time, and to list all those which are known would result in a daunting, academic work of thousands of pages. Instead, the book profiles the most common sources for the names involved.

At the same time the book gives a selection of the many other surnames which have much in common with the name under discussion. Sometimes, as in Roberts and Robertson, the connection is obvious, while in others – the connection between Richards and Dixon, for instance – the relationship may be surprising.

SURNAME SLEIGHT-OF-HAND

One of the many charms of the study of surnames is the surprises they yield. Some become extended by the addition of letters up front – the Welsh 'ap', the Irish 'O' and the Scottish 'Mac' are classic examples; while others have their extensions tacked on at the end – 'son' and 'ton' are two common examples.

Some names take on pretensions via hyphens and the like, while others shed letters, and indeed syllables.

Yet another group of names are positively acrobatic in their ability to do about-turns, while still others have a perverse quality of meaning the exact opposite of what you would expect (many Kings, for instance, do not come from royal roots).

ODDITIES

A 'miscellany' follows each history. As its name implies, this section provides a selection of interesting facts. You'll find murderers and millionaires, explorers and eccentrics, saints and sinners, nicknames and all sorts of fascinating information.

Next is a listing of places around the world which are similarly named, giving cities, towns, rivers, lakes, mountain ranges and islands which are namesakes.

NAMES AND NUMBERS

At the end of every name entry the book deals with the numbers involved for each name. The team of researchers for this book worked with a variety of sources to compile this information. These include census figures, Public Record Office data, regional experts and foreign governments. All figures quoted are, as near as possible, for 1980.

Compiling this section was not without its headaches, and itemising the figures for Ireland proved a large stumbling block. The problem here can be simply stated: the last census was countrywide and it occurred in 1890.

That would seem to rule out inclusion of any Irish figures. However, there are certain mitigating factors. The first is in many ways the most remarkable. Over the intervening ninety-plus years, Ireland's population has remained virtually constant. In 1890 the entire country had a population of 4,717,959, while the projected 1980 figure is 4,688,462 – a net loss of 29,497 over the period.

Thus assuming that the population has emigrated, died and been born in relation to those numbers (a very 'iffy' assumption as any demographer would tell you!), one can project from these ancient figures. It is far from perfect, but it was felt that giving rough estimates would be better than giving nothing at all.

Next there's the whole challenge of calculating which names occur the most frequently. England and Wales issue a list of the top fifty surnames, while Scotland provides the top hundred. Although the lists overlap, they are far from identical.

Then, too, some areas count spelling variants in with the basic surname – a final 'e', for instance – while others do not. Thus, on occasions, the book shows separate counts for separate spellings whilst elsewhere this has not been possible. The United States are the greatest offenders in this respect. Martins may be amused to learn that they are lumped with the Martinez's.

As far as is known the city-by-city information is the first of its kind. To compile this information the team analysed available telephone directories to determine the number of subscribers who hold a surname, then compared that number with the total number of subscribers in the same area. They then projected that number to cover the total population of the area concerned. This technique makes two big assumptions: that those not on the telephone occur in the population with the same frequency as those who are; and that their family sizes are similar. It isn't ideal but it is a pretty fair estimate.

Again a caveat is necessary. In South Africa far more whites than blacks are on the telephone, so our projections to total urban areas there doubtless overstate the case for those cities.

All of the above just goes to show that the world of demography, like the world of etymology, is strewn with minefields.

A FINAL WORD

The most famous of the Marx brothers is reputed to have said, 'Groucho isn't my real name. I'm just breaking it in for a friend'. This book looks at real names, our names, one of the few things which remain constant throughout our lifetime. It is hoped that the pages which follow will tell you more about your own name and about those of friends, with some surprises and amusement along the way.

THE ORIGINS OF SURNAMES

With rare exceptions, virtually all British surnames are based on or have grown from one (or very occasionally more) of fourteen starting points. Where our ancestors lived and what they looked like, their work and their hobbies all played a part in forming the surnames which surround us today.

Sometimes the association is direct, as in Baker or Fisher, though even here one encounters amusing subtleties. For example, most villages had one baker, one smith, one cooper, so these names can accurately describe what an ancestor did. Fisher is a totally different matter. Those who lived by the sea were never called Fisher for a good reason: because so many men in the area earned their living in this manner hopeless confusion would have resulted if the name had been in general use. Only when a fisherman moved inland was he so designated in honour of the curiosity value of his former profession.

Here then are the fourteen different areas which have given rise to our British names:

THE ORIGINS

Names derived from first names or patronymics

This category accounts for by far the largest number of modern names. Common examples here are: Jones, Nixon, Fitzhugh, McDonald, Johnson, Jackson, Wilson, Robinson, Tomlinson, Simpson, Dixon, Dickinson.

Names derived from other relations

Examples here are Eames, which means son of an uncle; Neave, the medieval word for nephew; Cousins, Godson, Kinderson.

Names derived from physical characteristics

Some of the most obvious examples here are Beard,

Whitehead, Brown, Redd and Reed, Long, Short, Small, Longfellow, Dark, Goodbody, Dunn (meaning 'dark').

Names derived from traits

Not only were some of our forebears named for their appearance, others bore labels describing their personalities or actions. Among these names one finds, for instance, Giddy, Swift, Hardy, Goodpastor (note the profession hiding there), Fox (as in 'smart as a –'), Smart, Worthy, Harty, Goodfellow, Gray, Moody (meaning brave), Wise, Keen, Bright, Pratt (meaning 'cunning').

Names derived from metaphor and ritual

Many of our ancestors took their names either from the way others regarded them or from roles they played in village pageants. Popular examples of these are King, Pope, Abbott, Lord, Duke, Priest.

Names derived from literature, myth and fable

The Bible is the all-time name generator here. Some examples are Aaron, Simons, Peters, Johns, Matthews, Joseph, Luke, Jude and Thomas.

Names derived from occupations

Smith is the champion in this category, but the world is full of those whose names tell us what their forefathers worked at. For example, Gardener, Skinner, Carter, Clark, Taylor, Fuller (one who 'fulled' cloth to clean it), Parson, Potter, Wright (including derivations such as Cartwright, Wheelwright and so forth), Archer, Miller, Weaver, Mason, Cooper, Glover, Goldsmith, Butcher, Chandler, Spicer, Sawyer, Draper, Waller, Slater, Spooner, Collier, Fisher, Brewer, Saddler, Carpenter, Baker (and Baxter), Farmer, Barber, Cook, Day (meaning 'dairyman'), Fowler.

Names derived from sayings

Once, England was full of hawkers proclaiming their wares, as exemplified by the street cries of London. Often the cry became the surname. Two examples of this type are Goodall – from 'Good Ale' – and Pardie – 'Per Deum' (for God).

Names derived from actions and events

Things which happened to our ancestors, or events in which they took part, can be reflected in the names we live with. Among names of this type are Drum, Shakespeare (a spear-bearer), Voyager, Conquest.

Names associated with animals and plants

Some families took their name from the everyday animals and plants with which they came in contact such as Salmon, Apple, Rose, Vine, Bull.

Names which indicate nationality

Long before passports, many of us bore names which stated where we came from. Among these are English, French, Norman, Saxon, Fleming, Dennis (meaning Danish).

Names associated with a man-made landmark

In the absence of a numbered street address, it was often handy to have a name which helped direct people to you, especially in larger towns. Examples of this kind of name include Bridges, Bell, Castle, Hall, Street, Towers.

Names associated with natural landmarks

In rural areas nature itself gave rise to an enormous number of names like, for instance, Banks, Ford, Rivers, Holloway, Westbrook, Grove, Brooks, Downs, Field, Moore.

Names which are status-oriented

Names of this type are largely medieval and derive from positions in the feudal hierarchy. Among the more frequent examples of this type are Squire, Sargeant, Bailey, Butler, Chamberlain, Ward (and Warden, Warder), Knight, Page, Marshall.

ALLAN ALLEN

RELATED NAMES

Other surnames which are related as to root, derivation or usage include:

Alain	Aleyn	Allenby	Alleyne
Alan	Allain	Allens	FitzAlan
Alano	Allanson	Alleyn	FitzAllan
	FitzAllen	Van Allen	

The surname Allen also occurs as Allan, Alleyne, Allain and derives from the popular first name Alan which also gives rise to FitzAlan. The origins of the name remain uncertain. It is possible that it derives from 'the Alan', meaning a member of the nomadic Scythian tribe which emerged from Central Asia in the centuries before the birth of Christ. The first references to the name are found in early Breton ballads. Here the name occurs in the form 'Alamn'. The name soon standardised to Alan in Old Breton and Alain in Old French, though it remained a Breton name. Its popularity increased as a result of one Alan, Bishop of Quimper, a Welsh-Breton, whose holy life led him to become the first St Alan. It is perhaps from the example of St Alan that it was said in those days that the name Alan meant 'harmony', though this remains unconfirmed from etymological sources.

The name Alan first came to England with the Norman Conquest. Amongst William the Conqueror's companies in arms were several Alans (and Alains), notably Alain le Roux (Alan the Red). After the Conquest, along with several other Breton first names, the first name Alan became widespread in England. Several remain popular as surnames to this day. Examples include Brett, Jewell, Brian, Justin and Wymark.

Curiously, the first name Alan became most popular in England in its Old French form of Alain, rather than the Old Breton form of Alan. In the centuries after the Conquest this name was found most frequently in Lincolnshire, where many of William the Conqueror's Breton soldiers settled as farmers. The first recorded English mention of the surname dates from the earliest records of the Domesday Book which record a certain Alanus in Suffolk in 1086. This is the Latinised form of the name; the additional '-us' may well have been little more than a clerical formalisation (Latin being the prevalent written language of the time). The name also appears in this form in the Domesday records for Lincolnshire in 1150.

The name Allen as a surname, and as a first name (with various spellings in both cases), is also popular in Scotland, though there is no question of Breton links in these cases as this part of Britain was not subject to Norman conquest. Here the name derives from the Gaelic personal name Ailin, from 'ail' – 'stone'. It may thus be originally a place name – for a man who lived by, or under a large, prominent stone or rock; or in some cases it may have been a nickname, attributing stoniness – either of strength, or character, or brain – to its owner. These early nicknames were often the result of local wit – and were often ironic – the local Alan (or stone) could therefore frequently have been not the village Sampson, but rather the village simpleton or weakling.

As Allan (the most frequent Scottish form) this name is often found in Northumbria. Here some of the derivations are doubtless from the Breton, though the large majority are of Scottish (Gaelic) origin.

AN ALLEN MISCELLANY

Allens can take pride in two of Ireland's most notable geographic features – the Bog of Allen, over 378 square miles of peat bogs in East Central Eire; and Lough Allen, on the Shannon, which is 8 miles long and up to 3 miles wide.

*

Allen's rule is the zoological principle that cold-climate animals have shorter smaller appendages and thus keep body heat loss down. It is named after US zoologist, Joel Asaph Allen.

*

The surname boasts six Lord Mayors of London: Roger FitzAlan (1212–14), Peter FitzAlan (1246), Sir John Aleyn

(1525 and 1535), William Allen (1571) Thomas Alleyn (1659) and William Allen (1867).

*

The Van Allen radiation belts, 600 miles from the earth, have a major effect on our planet's atmosphere and rotation. They're named after their American discoverer, physicist James Alfred Van Allen (b. 1914–).

*

The British Field Marshal, Viscount Allenby, Edmund Henry Hynman (1861–1936), is best remembered today for his invasion of Palestine during World War I, when he captured Jerusalem. This led to the fall of Damascus, and ultimately Turkey itself. The Allenby Bridge, which today links Israel and Jordan across the Jordan River, is named after him.

*

There are 5 towns in the United Kingdom which contain either Allan or Allen in their names. These range from Allanaquoich to Allensmore. The United States has 5 towns named Allen, along with another 8 towns which have Allen contained in their names. Both Syria and the United Kingdom have Allan Rivers, while New Zealand and the United States have Mount Allens.

*

With about 128,000 namesakes, Allen is the 39th most popular surname in England and Wales, while Allan, with about 16,000, is the 41st most popular surname in Scotland. Allen is notably popular in and around Leicester where an estimated one in about 300 families bears the name. In descending numerical order Nottingham, Sheffield and Birmingham are other Allen strongholds. Around the world, Allens are most common in Canberra (one in 500 families), Melbourne (one in 578) and Auckland (one in 680). The United States has more Allens than the entire population of Bristol – an estimated total of just over 480,000 makes this their 25th most popular name.

ANDERSON

RELATED NAMES

Other surnames which are related as to root, derivation or usage include:

Anders	Anderton	Andreas	Andrey
Andersen	Andison	Andress	Andris
Andersons	André	Andrew	Andrisoune
Andersson	Andrea	Andrewson	Androson

Endherson

Anderson is a modified form of Andrewson, meaning son of Andrew. Similar modifications and variations are fairly common amongst popular surnames, other widespread examples being Benson from Bennettson, Henderson from Henryson and, in certain cases, Alison from Allanson. Andrewson certainly passed through many forms before it finally became formulated as Anderson – this can be seen from the several 'in-between' derivatives which remain to this day (especially in Scotland). These include Andison (almost certainly derived from the shortened form of Andrew, Andy), Androson, Andrisoune, and even Endherson (though not Henderson which, as mentioned previously, comes from Henryson).

The first name Andrew comes from the Ancient Greek, where it means 'manly'. It has thus been in use for well over 2,000 years. The most famous Andrew is certainly one of the earliest recorded – St Andrew was Christ's first disciple. Legend has it that the remains of St Andrew were brought to Scotland in the fourth century by St Regulus. True or not, St Andrew is now firmly established as the patron saint and knightly champion of Scotland, his diagonal white cross featuring on the Scottish flag. Naturally enough, the name Andrew has long been popular in Scotland, its popularity first coming to the fore in the twelfth century. Thereafter, the name Anderson became prominent. Though the Scots haven't had it all their own way; the most concentrated populations of Andrews are found in the West Country, in Cornwall and Devon, while concentrations of Andersons are found slightly further east in Dorset and Hampshire.

The earliest British mention of any name connected with Andrew or Anderson is in the Domesday Book, where a certain Andreas is mentioned in 1086. It is nearly 200 years later before the first Andersons begin to make their recorded appearance. In the early-fifteenth-century Scottish records there are several Andrewsons and Androsouns, while in England, in the venerable-sounding *Register of the Guild of the Corpus Christi of the City of York*, one Androson appears in 1455 and an Androwson in 1482.

Owing to its popularity in Scotland, the name Anderson has proliferated wherever Scots have emigrated. This accounts for the large number of Andersons in New Zealand, Canada, and the United States. However, many of the American Andersons are of Swedish origin (Anderson is the most prevalent name in the Stockholm telephone directory.)

To a lesser degree, Andersons are indigenous all over Europe. The origin of the name is the same, and its pan-European popularity undoubtedly stems from St Andrew (who was also patron saint of Russia). The name Andrew has many European forms – ranging from the French André (as in the French writer/philosopher, André Malraux) to the German Andreas (as in Andreas Baader, of the notorious Baader–Meinhof Gang). Curiously, despite the name's popularity, there have been no major European kings called Andrew. Neither Scotland nor England has had a King Andrew, though the Queen's second son is so named. Also, there have been no popes named Andrew.

AN ANDERSON MISCELLANY

Andersons have been involved in a number of record-breaking crimes. George 'Dutch' Anderson pulled off a 1921 mail van stick-up which yielded over £500,000; Charlie Anderson took part in the first Wild West train robbery (1866); and 'Boston Pete' Anderson successfully talked a reclusive miser out of £850,000 in 1866 and sensibly retired.

*

The Anderson Shelter, invented by one-time British

Chancellor of the Exchequer John Anderson, was a simple affair which could easily be installed (as over 3 million were) in a back garden. It saved countless lives during World War II air raids.

*

Andersen's disease is one of five types of hereditary glycogen-storage diseases. Metabolic problems affect the liver, spleen, muscles and lymph nodes, the liver ultimately deteriorates and the patient dies.

*

Andersonville Prison in Sumter County, Georgia, was notorious during America's Civil War. In the two years of its existence (1864–5) this log stockade of at most 26 acres housed over 32,000 Northern prisoners, half of whom died.

*

Andersons have long figured prominently in the arts. Hans Christian Andersen (1805–75) created some of the world's best-loved fairy tales. America's Sherwood Anderson (1876–1941) and Maxwell Anderson (1888–1959) were prize-winning poets and novelists, while Marian Anderson (b.1902) is a famed black opera star.

*

There are towns called Anderson in the United Kingdom, Argentina and the United States, rivers of this name in Canada and the United States, and islands so named in Canada and Australia.

*

With about 38,000 namesakes, Anderson is Scotland's 8th most popular surname. Thus about one out of every 140 Scots is named Anderson. (The name is not common enough throughout England and Wales to be counted separately.) Anderson is notably popular in and around Edinburgh, where an estimated one in about 120 families bears the name, and in Glasgow where the figure is about one in 160. Around the world, Andersons are most common in Vancouver (one in 290 families), Wellington (one in 410), Auckland (one in 420) and Melbourne (one in 425). The United States has more Andersons than the entire population of Glasgow – an estimated total of just over 867,000 makes this their 9th most popular surname.

BAILEY

RELATED NAMES

Other surnames which are related as to root, derivation or usage include:

Baile	Baillie	Bayle	Baylis
Baileff	Bailly	Bayless	Bayliss
Bailie	Baily	Bayley	Baylot
Bailiff	Bally	Baylies	Bayly

Over half a dozen variations of the name remain in common use. These range from Baillie and Bayly to Baylis and Bayless.

Bailey is an occupational name deriving from the Old French words 'abillif' and 'baillis'. In medieval times a bailiff was anything from a Crown official to a King's officer in a town or county, a keeper of a Royal household, or simply a Sheriff's deputy. On feudal estates he was often a manorial official of some importance. For instance, the medieval records for the Manor of Droxford show the bailiff as receiving no less than the sum of £6 per annum – whereas the ploughman received only 8 shillings: a mere 1/15th of the bailiff's wage (the poor shepherds received only 4 shillings). What's more, the bailiff lived in the manor house at his lord's expense. For this princely wage, he acted as a kind of agricultural supervisor-cum-foreman for his lord's estate. His task was to make sure that the lands were properly and efficiently farmed, and to allot tasks to the workers. If a feudal lord was lazy or away at the Crusades, the bailiff virtually ran the estate. Thus he was a key man in its financial success or failure.

The name Bailey came across to England with William the Conqueror – probably in its original form of Bailiff. The origins of this name remain obscure, though it is possible that it derives from the Ancient Roman word for a burden – bajalus. Thus, a bailiff would be a person who bore a burden, or responsibility. The first English mention of the name Bailey appears in the thirteenth century. It is mentioned in the *Friar's Tale* by Chaucer (' "Artow then a bayley?" "Ye", quod he.'); Harry Bailey was the name of the Host in Chaucer's *Canterbury Tales*. The name also appears in the Hundred Rolls of 1273, where a certain Alvered Ballivus (the Latinised form) appears in the records for Lincolnshire.

The name Bailey is also common in Scotland, where a Scots alderman is still referred to as a bailie. The earliest Scottish mention comes in the 1311–13 records for Lothian, where one William de Baillie appears as a juror. The 'de' means this name almost certainly refers to a place, probably a keep or castle. In Lancashire also the surname Bailey appears as de Baylegh (1246), from the place Bailey (near Stonyhurst), a name meaning 'glade where berries grow'.

During this time, and in subsequent centuries, there was some confusion about the name Bailey (or Baillie and so on) in Scotland. According to popular Clydeside myth all Baileys had originally been called Balliol, but changed their names because of the two unpopular Scottish kings of that name. In most instances this was not the case.

A BAILEY MISCELLANY

In medieval times a bailey was a fort surrounded by a deep ditch and protected on the inside by a wooden palisade.

*

The Old Bailey, London's Central Criminal Court, is named for the street in which it stands, whose name in turn derives from the days when a medieval fort stood on the location which was just outside the City's walls.

*

The Bailey Bridge invented by Sir Donald Bailey was first used in 1942–3. Made of uniform prefabricated girders, it was easy to transport and erect, yet strong enough to bear tanks or trains.

*

The Baily Cup (1920 on) is the top prize in British Amateur Real Tennis doubles.

*

Baily's beads, named for their discoverer Francis Baily (1774–1844), are seen during an eclipse of the sun. Just before total eclipse, the narrow crescent of the sun's rays is broken by the moon's mountains and valleys. Seen from the earth, this gives a bead-like effect.

*

Since 'baile' means town in Gaelic, Ireland abounds in the name and in the corruption 'Bally', such as Ballycastle and Ballyshannon. Baile Atha Cliath (town at the ford of the hurdles) is Dublin's official Gaelic name.

*

The only town to bear a version of this surname in the United Kingdom is Bailleston. However, there are two Baileys in the United States and South Africa also has a town so named.

*

With about 107,000 namesakes, Bailey is the 49th most popular surname in England and Wales. (The name is not common enough throughout Scotland to be counted separately.) Bailey is notably popular in and around Leicester where an estimated one in about 390 families bears the name. In descending numerical order Manchester, Sheffield and Bristol are other Bailey strongholds. Around the world Baileys are most common in Montreal (one in 683 families), Canberra (one in 1,000) and Sydney (one in 1,122). The United States has more Baileys than the entire population of Plymouth – an estimated total of just over 275,000 makes this their 60th most popular surname.

BAKER

RELATED NAMES

Other surnames which are related as to root, derivation or usage include:

Bachuss Backster Bakker Bullinger
Backhouse Backus Baxter Pestor
Pillinger Pistor Pullinger

Like many other widespread English names, Baker is an occupational name, Brewer and Taylor being two other common examples. The name Baker derives from the Old English word 'baecere', for the man who worked in the 'baechus' (bakehouse).

Throughout history the baker has played an important part in community life. According to feudal law, peasants (or serfs) were allowed to grind corn only at their lord's mill. Likewise, they were allowed to bake only at their lord's oven. Thus the village oven became a vital part of the community, and its overseer was a personage of some importance. Soon the name 'baecere' acquired many variations. The fourteenth-century Midlands poet, Langland (author of *Piers Plowman*), mentions 'bakesteres' and 'brewesteres'. This form contains the female suffix -ester as in spinster (compare spinner), a more recognisable modern form. Later, this feminine form became standardised as Baxter or Backster – two names which remain widespread to this day.

Names related to the original 'baechus' include Backhouse, Bachuss and Backus. (Contrary to popular myth, these last two names have nothing whatsoever to do with the Greek god Bacchus or any nickname stemming from associated bibulous characteristics.)

Other names which are synonymous with Baker include Bullinger, Pullinger and Pillinger, from the Old French 'boulenger' which means 'baker', and Pistor and Pestor, Latin translations which were felt to have snob appeal.

As the centuries passed, the public baker became an

integral part of medieval urban life. As with many other trades, bakers would often congregate on one street. This sometimes accounts for the occurrence in towns of street names like Baker Street and Baxter Street.

One of the first mentions of this name comes in the Norfolk Pipe Rolls of 1177, where one William le Bakere is listed. By the time of the Hundred Rolls of 1273, the name was being listed all over the country – from Walter le Baker in Devon to Alan le Baker in Sussex. This year also saw the first listing of the feminine form; in the Rolls for Norfolk one John le Bakestere is listed.

A BAKER MISCELLANY

London's Baker Street is named after the manager of the Portmans' Marylebone Estates, William Baker. He leased fields for building.

*

221B Baker Street was Sherlock Holmes's address, according to Sir Arthur Conan Doyle. The number doesn't actually exist but a building society which has the nearest real address receives thousands of letters sent to Holmes each year.

*

London's Bakerloo Underground line is so named because originally it ran from Baker Street to Waterloo.

*

'The Baker' was the derisory nickname given to Louis XVI after he and Marie Antoinette (known as 'the Baker's Wife' ever after, which wasn't long) dispensed bread to the rioting mobs at Versailles in 1789.

*

Robert Baker was a seventeenth-century London tailor whose collar borders were called pickadillies, the origin of Piccadilly. The land he willed to his two sons, John and James, is also commemorated today as Upper and Lower John and James Streets.

*

The 'Baker Flying' is a red flag used by the US Navy to warn those in the vicinity to stay well clear when a dangerous operation such as loading ammunition is under way.

*

A Baker's Dozen is 13 rolls for the price of 12, as well as being a nickname for the 13th Hussars.

*

The London livery company, the Worshipful Company of Bakers, dates from 1486.

*

Bakers are geographically well represented. The UK has towns called Baker's End and Baker Street. No fewer than 8 US states have towns called Baker, and there are 3 Bakersfields as well. The United States also oversees an uninhabitable South Pacific Baker Island which was once British. Canada, Australia and the United States have Baker Lakes, while Chile has a Baker Canal.

*

With about 145,000 namesakes Baker is the 31st most popular surname in England and Wales. (The name is not common enough throughout Scotland to be counted separately.) Baker is notably popular in and around Bristol where an estimated one in about 275 families bears the name. In descending numerical order Birmingham, Cardiff and Leicester are other Baker strongholds. Around the world Bakers are most common in Sydney (one in 638 families), Canberra (one in 657) and Auckland (one in 723). The United States has more Bakers than the entire population of Bristol – an estimated total of just under 433,000 makes this their 33rd most popular surname.

BENNETT

RELATED NAMES

Other surnames which are related as to root, derivation or usage include:

Ben	Benn	Benniman	Benns
Bence	Bennet	Bennison	Benny
Benedict	Bennetts	Bennitt	Benoit
Benét	Bennie	Bennitts	Bense
	Benson	Benyson	

The name Bennett comes from the first name Benedict. This name originates from the Latin word 'benedictus' which means 'blessed' – a popular Christian name in late Roman times. It was also the name of the fifth-century founder of the Benedictine Order. Since that time, no fewer than fifteen popes have taken the name Benedict.

With the decay of Latin, the popular name Benedict was adapted into many languages. In Italian it became Benedetto, in French Benoit. The French form came to England with the Norman Conquest, then gradually evolved to Bennett. In the process many variations arose, some of which remain in common use today. Bennetts, for instance, means 'dependant of Bennett'; Benson means 'son of Bennett', if it is not the alternative surname derived from the place in Oxfordshire. The surname Benn also derives from the old source (and, so far as we can tell, not from *Ben*jamin). The variation Bennet is usually found in the north of the country.

The records of Furness Abbey, which was run by the Benedictine Order, indicate a great number of baptisms with the names of Bennet and Benson. Indeed, these names (the two most popular forms) are found to be particularly prevalent in areas where the Benedictine monks flourished. Other variations found in Benedictine baptismal records include the names Bennison, Benns, Bence, Bense, Bennie and Benny.

The earliest reference to a Bennett is in the 1193 records

for Oseney Abbey. Here the name appears as Beneit, which is a variation of the Old French form. The earliest Bensons appear in the 1326 Rolls of Wakefield Manor, where John Benneson and Adam Bensome are listed. A rare variation of the name appears in Shakespeare. In *Much Ado About Nothing* one of the characters is called Benedick.

Bennett remained for many years a popular first name, but it is now rare. Likewise, the *first* name Ben is nowadays usually short for Benjamin, rather than for Benedict. Thus Bennett curiously remains a popular surname which derives from an original first name now almost unused.

A BENNETT MISCELLANY

Bennettitales is an alternative name for an extinct species of palm-like plants which constituted a major portion of the earth's vegetation during the middle Mezozoic period some 150 million years ago.

*

Bennett's Fracture is a fracture of the base of the thumb, named in honour of Edward Hallaron Bennett, the eminent Irish physician who was an expert on breaks and dislocations.

*

The geographical term 'ben' comes from the Gaelic word for peak (beann). Thus parts of Britain – especially Scotland and Ireland – abound in mountains incorporating the word: Ben Nevis, for instance, and Ben More.

*

There are no United Kingdom towns incorporating the name Bennett. Australia and the United States have Bennett mountains while New Zealand has a Cape Bennett.

*

With about 117,000 namesakes, Bennett is the 46th most popular surname in England and Wales. (The name is not common enough throughout Scotland to be counted separately.) Bennett is notably popular in and around Birmingham where an estimated one in about 420 families bears the name. In descending numerical order Bristol, Sheffield and Liverpool are other Bennett strongholds. Around the world Bennetts are most common in Sydney (one in 719 families), Canberra (one in 767) and Auckland (one in 805). The United States has more Bennetts than the entire population of Southampton – an estimated total of just under 255,000 makes this their 69th most popular surname.

BROWN

RELATED NAMES

Other surnames which are related as to root, derivation or usage include:

Broun	Brownett	Brownsmith	Bruin
Broune	Browning	Brownson	Brunet
Browne	Brownjohn	Brownutt	Brunsen
	Brunson		

The name Brown is an old colour-name which is a form of nickname. Colour-names usually referred to the complexion or hair of the owner. There are several common names which began life as colour-names. Thus the name Reed, Reid (or Read) derives from the Old English word 'read' which means 'red'. Similarly, Blake is thought in most cases to derive from the Old English word 'blac' which means 'black'; and Blunt derives from the Middle English word 'blund', meaning 'white' or 'fair-haired'.

The name Brown derives from the Old English word 'brun', meaning 'brown', though in some cases it may derive from a foreign version of the same word. The name Brown, in the form Brun, was certainly prevalent throughout the country before the Norman Conquest. However, a number of Bruns came across the Channel with William the Conqueror so, in some cases, the name Brown derives from the French root (the modern French word for brown is 'brun').

In the 1066 records of the Domesday Book we find reference to one Brun, and the Latinised form Brunus. These were personal names. However, by 1273 we find the surname form with Hugh le Brun in Suffolk and Robert le Brun in Buckinghamshire.

Naturally enough, such a simple and widespread name soon acquired many variations, several of which remain in use to this day. Brownett and Brunet are diminutives of the Old French Brun. Browning represents Old English Bruning, from the Old English Brun – in the same way as Dunning or

Downing from Dunn, 'the dark, swarthy or dun-coloured one'. Brownutt comes from a medieval nickname describing its owner as 'brown as a nut'. Brownsmith comes from the Old English 'brun' and 'smith', meaning 'a worker in copper or brass'. The names Brownson and Brunson simply mean 'son of Brown'. And Brownjohn derives from an old medieval nickname meaning 'John with the brown hair (or face)'.

For many years Brown has been Scotland's third most numerous surname – after Smith and McDonald. However, some Scottish Browns may derive their name from a different source from their English counterparts. In England the name usually comes from the Old English, or sometimes from the Old French, but in Scotland and parts of the north of England, the name may sometimes come from the Old Scandinavian 'Brúnn' – a subtle distinction, but it spreads the origins of the Browns from Norway to Brittany.

A BROWN MISCELLANY

Brown vs Board of Education of Topeka, Kansas (1954) was a landmark decision of the United States Supreme Court which marked the beginning of the end of segregation. The Court ruled that 'separate but equal' educational facilities for people of different races were inherently unequal, and thus violated the US Constitution's 14th Amendment, which guarantees all citizens equal protection under the law.

*

The cross-the-chest military fashion called the Sam Browne belt is named after General Sir Samuel Jones Browne (1824–1901) who made it popular.

*

Brownies have long been fairies in Scotland and Eire, while around the English-speaking world they are the descriptive term for the youngest group of Girl Guides. Their name derives from their uniform.

*

Browns have been exceptionally inventive on both sides of the Atlantic. Inventions include all sorts of precision instruments (Joseph Rogers Brown – USA, 1810–76), armour plate (Sir John Brown – UK, 1816–96), hoisting and conveying machines (Alexander Ephraim Brown – USA,

1852–1911), the Browning submachine gun and numerous other firearms (John Moses Brown – USA, 1855–1926), and the gyroscopic compass and aeroplane speed indicator (Sydney George Brown – UK, 1873–1948).

*

Brownian Motion, the common term for the rapid oscillating movement of particles suspended in liquid or gas which, when viewed through a microscope, is evidence of molecular motion, is named after the Scots-born botanist, Robert Brown (1773–1858).

*

Six Lord Mayors of London have had a Brown-related surname: Stephen Broun (1438), John Browne (1480), William Browne (1507), William Browne (1513), Sir Richard Browne (1660) and Anthony Brown (1826).

*

Browns have been notable warriors in exotic places. Admiral William Brown (1777–1857) led the Argentinian fleet to two famous victories over the Brazilians. George Browne served the Czars, was enslaved in Turkey, escaped with state secrets, commanded the Russian Armies during the Danish War and retired to become the much revered Governor of Livonia in the Baltic for over 30 years.

*

As a colour-related name, towns and geographic features which contain the name Brown are frequent. The United Kingdom alone has 7 towns ranging from Brown Candover to Brownston while the United States has no fewer than 27 towns which contain the name. Australia has mountains called Browne and Brown, a peak named Brown Hills and a Brown Point.

*

With about 441,000 namesakes, Brown is the 4th most popular surname in England and Wales. There are over 49,000 Browns in Scotland where it is 3rd in popularity, while in Ireland it is estimated that with about 15,000 Browns it is the 37th most popular surname. Brown is notably popular in and around Edinburgh where an estimated one in about 85 families bears the name. In descending numerical order, Glasgow, Teesside and Nottingham are other

Brown strongholds. Around the world Browns are most common in Canberra (one in 202 families), Sydney (one in 231) and Auckland (one in 244). The United States has more Browns than the entire population of Birmingham and Coventry combined – an estimated total of just over 1,430,000 makes this their 4th most popular surname.

BYRNE

RELATED NAMES

Other surnames which are related as to root, derivation or usage include:

Björn	Byram	Byron	O'Biorain
Braniff	Byrnes	MacBrann	O'Birn
Brann	Byrns	MacBrannan	O'Boirne
Brannan	Byrom	MacBrinn	O'Brani
	O'Broin	O'Byrne	

The surname Byrne almost certainly has two derivations, while it has also spawned many variations.

The first derivation is from the Irish O'Birn. This means 'a descendant of Biorn', a name which came to Ireland with the Norse invaders. In Old Norse this name is written Björn, and it remains unchanged in modern Scandinavia, as in Björn Björg. Bjõrn originally meant 'bear' and was probably a descriptive nickname pertaining either to the appearance or to the fighting qualities of its holder.

The other derivation of Byrne is from the Irish O'Broin, which means 'a descendant of Bran'. In Old Irish 'bran' meant 'raven'. Thus originally this was probably a descriptive name or nickname, alluding either to the appearance or to some hoped-for quality of its holder. So, it is probable that many original Brans had very dark hair.

Through the centuries Byrne has been a major family name in East Leinster, and Byrnes have traditionally played a major role in resistance to English rule in Ireland.

Apart from the surname Byrne, there are many variations derived from the original Irish word 'bran'. These include such names as MacBrinn (son of Brinn) and MacBrann (found mostly in County Clare). Braniff and O'Brani derive from the Irish Brandinbh, which is made up of the Irish words 'bran' (raven) and 'dubh' (black). This name is found mainly in County Down. The name Brann occurs in East Ulster. Another variation is MacBrannan, or Brannan, which is distinct from the more common name Brennan, whose roots are entirely different.

In rare cases Byrne has a purely English derivation. Byrne and Byron are variants for the place names Byram (a township in the parish of Brotherton in Yorkshire) and Byrom (a small settlement near Winwick in Lancashire). This rare derivation of the name Byrne goes back many centuries, the first mention of it occurring in the Feet of Fines for Yorkshire (1240), where one Roger de Birum is listed. It is reported by Woulfe that Byram and Byron were sometimes used as English substitutes for Irish O'Byrne, etc, but most of the Byrams and Byrons are in fact derived from the Yorkshire and Lancashire place names.

A BYRNE MISCELLANY

The colourful Irish adventurer Miles Byrne (1780–1862), had one of the most unusual military careers of the nineteenth century. After joining the unsuccessful Irish rising which was defeated at the Battle of Vinegar Hill, he fled into hiding in the Wicklow Mountains. Here he met the great Irish leader Robert Emmet, who sent him to Paris to raise support. Napoleon gave Byrne a commission, and he then served with distinction in several of Bonaparte's famous campaigns. Byrne was eventually made Chef de Bataillon and given the Legion of Honour. Today a monument marks his tomb in Montmartre cemetery.

*

Contrary to popular misconception, Scotland's national poet 'Rabbie' Burns (1759–86), (author of 'Auld Lang Syne'), is not a Byrne. His name comes from Burness. The emphasis in this name is on the first syllable and 'Rabbie's' family shortened it to Burns.

*

One of the stars of the Women's Lib movement in America is Jane Byrne. In 1979 she took on the powerful Democratic Party system in Chicago and to the surprise of the pundits was elected the first woman Mayor of one of America's toughest cities.

*

The most celebrated of Romantic poets was Lord Byron

(1788–1824). His long autobiographical poem, *Childe Harold's Pilgrimage*, brought him fame and fortune. His subsequent notorious behaviour led him to live in self-imposed exile, in Switzerland and in Italy, where he met Shelley and Keats, and where he wrote his great satiric epic, *Don Juan.* He finally died while on an expedition to Greece to fight against the Turks for Greek independence.

*

Byrness in Northumbria is the only town containing the word Byrne.

*

In England, Scotland and Wales Byrne is not common enough to be counted separately. In Ireland, with about 35,000 namesakes, Byrne is the 7th most popular surname. Around the world Byrnes are most common in Auckland (one in 618 families) and in Sydney (one in 874). In the United States there are an estimated 32,000 Byrnes – making this their 991st most popular surname.

CAMPBELL

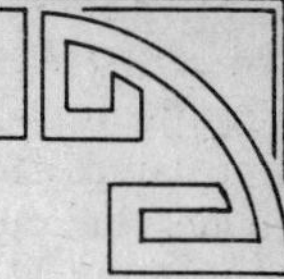

RELATED NAMES

Other surnames which are related as to root, derivation or usage include:

Camble Camel Cammel

The Campbells are Scotland's largest clan, though historically speaking they remain under something of a cloud for their notorious part in the Glencoe Massacre of the MacDonalds.

The surname Campbell originated as a nickname. The word Campbell comes from the Scots Gaelic 'caimbeul', which means 'wry (or crooked) mouth'. This is much the same as the origin of the name Cameron, which comes from the Scots Gaelic for 'wry (or crooked) nose'. These nicknames almost certainly referred to an element of character rather than just appearance.

According to the tradition of the Clan Campbell, the Campbells were originally known as 'Clann Duibhne' or 'O'Duine' and were descended from one Diarmed O'Duine of Lochow. Diarmed, in his turn, was said to be a direct descendant of the great Diarmed, 'the Fingalean hero who slew the wild boar'. Curiously, the father of this Diarmed was known as Fergus Cerr-beoil or Fergus the Wry-mouth, and it is just possible that the name Campbell originates from this. There is no Gaelic equivalent for the Clan Campbell, it still being referred to as Clann O'Duibhne, after Diarmed O'Duine.

Apart from these meagre facts, origins of the Clan Campbell are lost in mythology. The name appears in many ancient ballads and manuscripts, all of doubtful veracity. In one of these the Campbells are said to be descended from King Arthur, while another maintains that they are descended from Adam, no less.

The earliest mention of a Campbell comes in the Exchange Rolls for 1263, where one Gillespie Campbell is listed. However, even as late as 1447, we find in the manuscript

History of Craignish a man called Duncan le Campbell, where the name is used as a mere nickname. (Here the 'le' is not French, but denotes that what follows is vernacular. Loosely translated, the word means 'known as'.)

Despite the vague origins of the name Campbell, there is one popular myth which can be dismissed. Contrary to the legend, the Campbells are not of French origin, and the word Campbell is not derived from the Norman French 'de campobello' meaning 'of the beautiful plain'. If this were the case, the earliest listings of the name Campbell would be preceded by a 'de', as in the origins of such Norman French names as Beauchamp (now usually Beecham) meaning 'beautiful field'. There is no mention of any 'de Campbell'.

Campbell has few variations. The only notable ones are Camble, Camel, and Cammel. The last two forms are also in some cases descended from nicknames. A 'Camel' would be a large strong fellow capable of carrying great weights for a long distance, as we see in Shakespeare, who refers to 'a Dray-man, a Porter, and a very Camell'. There is also an etymological oddity attached to the name Camel. In the north-east of Scotland a pig was often known as a 'sandy camel', and this name passed to Holland, where it became 'kumpel'.

A CAMPBELL MISCELLANY

In the great age of world speed records, the Campbell family was the greatest of them all. Sir Malcolm Campbell (1885–1949) broke the world land-speed record nine times between 1924 and 1935, and later broke the water-speed record 3 times. His son Donald Campbell (1921–67) also broke both land and sea speed records several times and his tragic death while attempting a new water-speed record ended an era.

*

Britain's greatest linguist is George Campbell (b.1913). By the time he retired from the BBC Overseas Service he had mastered no fewer than 39 languages, although he admits that there was never a time when he could speak all 39, as he tended to grow rusty in one or two.

*

The girl nicknamed 'Highland Mary', who inspired many of Robbie Burns' greatest love lyrics, was almost certainly one Mary Campbell. There are now several statues to 'Highland Mary' in the Burns country around Greenock and Dunoon.

*

'The Campbells are coming' goes the famous refrain in the song – and one Campbell at least lived up to his name. One Robert Campbell, a fur trader, travelled over 3,000 miles from the Yukon to Montreal on snow shoes – an unparalleled feat. The Campbells can also sing. The queen of Britain's jazz singers, Cleo Laine (b.1928), the wife of bandleader Johnnie Dankworth, is in fact a Campbell. Her real name is Clementina Campbell.

*

The United Kingdom has a Campbelltown, a Campbelton and a Campbeltown. No fewer than 5 American states have towns named Campbell; so do Australia, South Africa and New Guinea.

*

With about 44,000 namesakes, Campbell is Scotland's 4th most popular surname; thus about one out of every 120 Scots is named Campbell. With over 16,000 Campbells, this is Ireland's 31st most popular surname. (The name is not common enough throughout England and Wales to be counted separately.) Campbell is notably popular in and around Glasgow where an estimated one in 101 families bears the name, and in Edinburgh (one in 160). Around the world Campbells are most common in Vancouver (one in 372 families), Wellington (one in 434) and Canberra (one in 442). The United States has more Campbells than the entire population of Coventry – an estimated total of just under 379,000 makes this their 41st most popular surname.

CARTER

RELATED NAMES

Other surnames which are related as to root, derivation or usage include:

Carters Cartier Cartwright Charter

The surname Carter was originally an occupational name, for a person who drove or made carts. ('Cart' is a diminutive from the same root as the word 'car', which originally meant 'conveyance'.) In early times carts were virtually the only form of overland transport of both goods and people; thus many original carters would have been as vital to everyday life as modern-day drivers of anything from lorries to taxis.

The origins of the word 'carter' are various depending on the basic form of the word for a cart in the derivation – Latin 'carettum', 'carettarius'; Old French 'charette', 'carette', etc. A related word, 'craet', was in use in England well before the Norman Conquest and there was also an Old Norse equivalent, 'kartr'. From these could well come English Carter. After the Norman Conquest, a French version was introduced – the Old French 'charetier', which originally meant 'chariot-driver'. (The well-known French name Cartier derives from a similar source.) This last derivation is probably responsible for the variant surname Charter, though most of the original French forms have been absorbed without trace into plain Carter. Another widespread derivative of cart is Cartwright (see Wright), which means 'a maker of carts'.

The earliest reference to the name Carter appears in the Latinised form. In the 1177 Pipe Rolls for Cambridgeshire one Fulco Carettarius is listed.

The French form of Carter, Cartier, could be confused with another series of French surnames, Cartier, Carteret, etc. ultimately from 'quartier' ('a quarter' – a measure for land and goods). Also the name Charter could be confused with Charters, Charteris or Chatteris, derived from Chartres in France or Chatteris in Cambridgeshire.

A CARTER MISCELLANY

Jewellers and gem merchants, Cartier, have, at one time or another, appraised the Topkapi collection, sold the Hope Diamond, the Romanov crown, a necklace given to Empress Marie-Louise by Napoleon, and the 69.4 carat pear-shaped Taylor–Burton diamond.

*

Tutankhamen's fourteenth-century BC royal tomb was discovered by British archaeologist Howard Carter (1873–1939). Probably the world's pre-eminent archaeological find, its treasures attracted unprecedented crowds when exhibited in Britain and America.

*

Jacques Cartier (1491–1557) was a famous French explorer who discovered Canada's St Lawrence River while looking for the fabled Northwest Passage to the Pacific. Believing he might have discovered it, he sailed down the river to the present site of Quebec, claiming the land for France as he went. As a result he might justifiably be identified as the source of Canada's separatist problems.

*

The United Kingdom has towns called Carter's Clay and Carterton. This latter name is also a town in New Zealand, while Australia has a Carter Mountain.

*

With about 104,000 namesakes, Carter is the 52nd most popular surname in England and Wales. (The name is not common enough throughout Scotland to be counted separately.) Carter is notably popular in and around Teesside where an estimated one in about 495 families bears the name. In descending numerical order Bristol, Bradford and Leicester are other Carter strongholds. Around the world Carters are most common in Auckland (one in 732 families), Sydney (one in 931), and Wellington (one in 949). The United States has more Carters than the entire population of Nottingham – an estimated total of just under 367,000 makes this their 43rd most popular surname.

CLARK

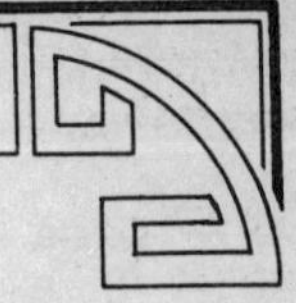

RELATED NAMES

Other surnames which are related as to root, derivation or usage include:

Clarke Clarkson Clarson Clerk
Clerke

Clarke is an occupational name, coming from the Old English 'clerec' or 'clerc' and the Old French 'clerc', both of which originate from the Latin 'clericus'.

The earliest Clarks were often clerics, ie clergymen or others in religious orders. In the Middle Ages literacy was largely confined to those in the Church, so most writing and secretarial work (including recording deaths, births, taxes and wills) was done by clerics or clergy.

As literacy grew and names became hereditary, the surname came to mean a scribe or administrative assistant who could draw up required papers. Thus did both the professional name 'clerk' and the surname Clarke catch on and endure.

Besides the obvious Clarkson (and the related Clarson) save in minor spelling alterations there are few variations of the name. The 'er' version, as in Clerke, is the more original version of the name. The 'er' often changed to 'ar'. A modern example is the way we pronounce Berkshire, Hertfordshire and Derbyshire. This change was fairly common. Other examples: 'varmint' (from the original 'vermin') and 'varsity' (from university).

The earliest mention of the name Clark is found in the Domesday Book for Hampshire. Here the records for 1086 mention one Richard Clericus.

A CLARK MISCELLANY

One of the most notorious royal mistresses of all time was Mary Anne Clarke (1776–1852). She became mistress to Frederick, Duke of York, George III's second son. Frederick was Commander-in-Chief of the Army, and Mary Anne used her position to secure promotion for several friends, accepting large bribes for her services.

*

The 'Trumpet Voluntary' is often mistakenly attributed to Purcell. In fact, it was composed by Jeremiah Clarke (1674–1707).

*

The only man to have won all 25 Grand Prix in the World Motor Racing Championship is James (Jim) Clark (1936–68). This he accomplished in 1965, breaking Fangio's record of 24. Clark died tragically in an accident at the Hockenheim circuit in West Germany.

*

During 1940 Colonel William Fredman and Harry Lawrence Clark managed to break the Japanese secret code. The code-breaker they created was nicknamed 'Magic' and it intercepted messages showing that the Japanese were planning to attack. Unfortunately, they were unable to discover the exact location of the attack – Pearl Harbor.

*

The first overland trip across the continent of North America set off in 1804 and was led by Captain Meriwether Lewis (1774–1809) and Lt William Clark (1770–1838), who acted as mapmaker and artist.

*

Clarkston is the only United Kingdom town with this name. However, throughout the Commonwealth the name Clark and variations on it are common both as town names and as names of geographic features. Clark's Harbour in Nova Scotia and Clark's Town in Jamaica are two examples. Some 21 towns and cities in the US are Clark-related.

*

With about 164,000 namesakes, Clarke is the 34th most popular surname in England and Wales while Clark accounts for another 136,000. In combination this makes the name the 8th most popular in the area. In Scotland about 25,000 Clarks makes this the 13th most popular name. Clark(e) is notably popular in and around Leicester where an estimated one in about 215 families bears the name. In descending numerical order other strongholds of one spelling or the other are Coventry, Nottingham, and Birmingham. Around the world Clarks and Clarkes are most common in Auckland (one in 238 families), Wellington (one in 292) and Melbourne (one in 336). In the United States there are an estimated 576,000 Clarks and 68,000 Clarkes, in combination making this the country's 15th most popular surname.

CONNOR

RELATED NAMES

Other surnames which are related as to root, derivation or usage include:

Connors O'Connor

Connor (or O'Connor) is an Irish surname. It derives from the Irish Gaelic 'Conchobhar'. Thus, O'Connor means 'the descendant of Conchobhar' (the descendant of 'high-will'). This refers to a quality in its possessor, just as the similar O'Connell refers to 'the descendant of Conale', or the descendant of 'high-powerful'.

Connor was the name of six entirely distinct leading families in Ireland and was found all over the country, though it was rare in Kerry.

Perhaps the most renowned of the six Connor families, or clans, originated in Connacht. This clan was called O'Connor or O'Connor Don. The last High King of Ireland came from this clan, which has many branches. Other O'Connor families include O'Connor Roe and O'Connor Sligo (from Sligo) and O'Connor Faly (from Offaly), as well as branches in Kerry and North Clare. All members of these branches can properly claim to be descended from kings.

The name Connor is sometimes confused with the completely English occupational name of Conner, which stems from the Old English word meaning 'inspector' or 'examiner'. Likewise, Connor (or O'Connor) has nothing to do with the similar but distinct Irish name of Connery (or O'Connery), which originated in Munster, mainly in and around Cork and Limerick.

A CONNOR MISCELLANY

At the 1906 Athens Olympics Irish Peter O'Connor won a gold medal for the Hop, Step and Jump. When the Union Jack was raised during the presentation of his medal, this so incensed O'Connor that, ignoring the ceremony in his honour, he descended the awards podium, climbed the flagpole and replaced the English flag with Ireland's own.

*

Ireland's best known short-story writer of this century was Michael O'Donovan (1901–66), who wrote under the name of Frank O'Connor. Called by Yeats 'the Irish Chekhov', he is best remembered for his stories about life in his native Cork, notably the collection *Crab Apple Jelly* (1944).

*

Rory O'Connor (1116–98), also known as Roderic, who was Turlough's son and the last High King of Ireland, failed to defeat the Anglo-Norman invasion which led to English rule. He retired to a monastery where he died.

*

Connor has few towns and geographic features named in its honour, but Australia does have a Mount Connor and a Connors Range.

*

In England, Scotland and Wales the name Connor is not common enough to be counted separately. In Ireland, with about 33,000 namesakes, Connor is the 9th most popular surname. Around the world Connors and O'Connors are most common in Canberra (one in 1,509 families), Sydney (one in 2,134) and Melbourne (one in 2,392). In the United States there are an estimated 57,000 Connors and 85,000 O'Connors, in combination making this the country's 168th most popular surname.

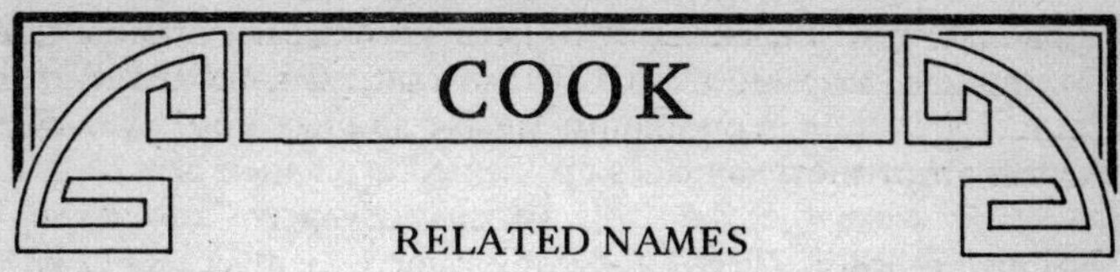

COOK

RELATED NAMES

Other surnames which are related as to root, derivation or usage include:

Coke	Cookes	Cooks	Cuckson
Cooke	Cookman	Cookson	Cuxon

Cook is an occupational surname from the Old English word 'coc'. Originally a cook might have been anything from a cook as we know it to a cooked-meat seller or even the keeper of an eating-house.

There are many variations on this surname from the obvious Cookson (which gives us Cuckson and Cuxon) to Cookes, Coke, and the more popular Cooke. Many commentators consider the final 'e' in Cooke as snobbish and affected. However, this is the spelling which is found in the fourteenth century from *Piers Plowman*, which refers to 'Brewester, Batess, Bochers and Cookes'.

After the Norman Conquest a French variation appeared. This is Lequeux, which despite its exotic appearance means simply 'cook'. It comes from the Old French word 'queu', meaning a 'cook', a 'seller of cooked meats', or an 'eating-house keeper'. (The strikingly similar English word 'queue' does not, however, come from this source. It comes from the Old French word for a tail – le queue – which may have been the origin of Kew Gardens. Alternatively, the name Kew sometimes derives from a place name, a (now vanished) town near Boulogne.)

Naturally, this good old English name for a vital activity abounds in ancient records. The earliest mention of the name comes over a century before the Domesday Book, in an Anglo-Saxon will dating from approximately 950, where one Aelfsige Se Coc is mentioned.

A COOK MISCELLANY

The explorations of Captain James Cook have left the name

Cook all over the Pacific Ocean. The two most notable geographical features named after this famous navigator are the Cook Islands in the South Pacific and Cook Strait, New Zealand. Many other places are named after members of his crew, or even the days on which they were discovered (Christmas Island, for instance).

*

To be given a 'Cook's Tour' of somewhere is to be shown round it, usually by a guide, and comes from the first great travel firm, Thomas Cook & Co, started in 1841.

*

The hat we today call a 'bowler' was introduced by one William Coke, a Norfolk huntsman, in 1850. Mr Coke asked his hatter, Mr Beaulieu of Nelson Square, London, to design him headgear more suitable than the then fashionable tall riding hat. The new hat became known as a bowler after the anglicisation of the designer's name, though at the beginning it was also often referred to as a 'Coke'.

*

The United Kingdom has 10 Cook-related towns – these range from Cookbury to Cookstown. Predictably the Pacific Ocean and Australia are full of Cooks including Cook Island, Mount Cooke, the Cook District of Canberra and a major reef in New Caledonia.

*

With about 102,000 namesakes Cook is the 53rd most popular surname in England and Wales. Were those with an 'e' at the end of the name added, the number and ranking would increase markedly. This variation is not common enough to be counted separately and neither version's count is available for Scotland for the same reason. Cook(e) is notably popular in and around Bristol where an estimated one in about 425 families bears the name. In descending numerical order other strongholds of one spelling or the other are Teesside, Birmingham and Cardiff. Around the world Cooks and Cookes are most common in Canberra (one in 561 families), Auckland (one in 639) and Wellington (one in 660). In the United States there are an estimated 313,000 Cooks and 38,000 Cookes, in combination making this the country's 43rd most popular surname.

COOPER

RELATED NAMES

Other surnames which are related as to root, derivation or usage include:

Cooperman Coopper Copper Couper
Cowper Cupere Cupper

The surname Cooper is an occupational name. It stems from the Middle English word 'coupere', meaning 'a maker or repairer of wooden casks, buckets or tubs'. The Middle English word derives from a Latin word, 'cuparius'.

In medieval times the occupation of cooper played a vital part in commercial and community life, for in those days all liquids were conveyed in tubs and barrels. The craft of coopering is still practised today to produce wooden barrels for real ale, whisky and port (and any other liquid to be 'matured in wood').

As is to be expected of such a widespread profession, the name Cooper is relatively evenly distributed all over the country, with the unaccountable exception of parts of the North. For this reason, there are many spelling variations. These include Couper, Cowper and even Cupper. Another variation is Copper, though in some cases this means 'worker in copper' (as in the variation Coppersmith). Another variation of Cooper is spelt Coopper, though it is now rare.

The earliest mention of this name occurs in the Pipe Rolls for Surrey of 1176–7. Here one Robert (le) Cupere is mentioned. The Pipe Rolls for Norfolk of 1181–2 also mention two le Cuperes. The French 'le' is strictly Norman, becoming widespread in England after the Conquest. It was particularly prevalent in occupational names – thus Robert the Cooper, Charles the Baker, and so on.

A COOPER MISCELLANY

The Worshipful Company of Coopers in the City of London was founded in 1501. This Livery Company maintained the standards of the trade, also supervising apprenticeships. Originally it was a guild which consisted of makers of all kinds of wooden casks and buckets, as well as barrels.

*

The Cooper is a famous British racing car. The first version was built in 1946 by John Cooper and his father, Charles. By 1955 the Cooper was a world-beater and, with Jack Brabham driving, won the Australian Grand Prix. From 1959 through the early 1960s the Cooper (now with a Coventry-Climax engine) dominated the Grand Prix field and won the World Championship.

*

The surname has long dominated the world's stages and cinemas. Notable thespians include Dame Gladys Cooper (1888–1971), Gary Cooper (1901–61), Lady Diana Cooper (b.1892) and Jackie Cooper (b.1921).

*

The United Kingdom has a Coopersdale Common and a town called Coopernook. The United States has 7 Cooper-related towns including Cooperstown, well known in America for its Baseball Hall of Fame. New Zealand has a Cooper Island while Canada and Australia have Cooper mountains.

*

With about 158,000 namesakes Cooper is the 27th most popular surname in England and Wales. (The name is not common enough throughout Scotland to be counted separately.) Cooper is notably popular in and around Sheffield where an estimated one in about 290 families bears the name. In descending numerical order Leicester, Nottingham and Birmingham are other Cooper strongholds. Around the world Coopers are most common in Sydney (one in 701 families), Auckland (one in 713) and Canberra (one in 719). The United States has more Coopers than the entire population of Leicester – an estimated total of just over 283,000 makes this their 57th most popular surname.

DAVIS DAVIES

RELATED NAMES

Other surnames which are related as to root, derivation or usage include:

Dakins	David	Daviss	Daw
Davage	Davideson	Davisson	Dawe
Daves	Davidge	Davitt	Dawes
Daveson	Davidson	Davson	Daweson
Davey	Davie	Davy	Dawkins
Daveys	Davison	Davys	Daws

Dawson

The surname Davis (or Davies) stems from the first name David, usually by way of the nickname Davy which was also the French popular form, much in use after the Norman Conquest. Davis means 'son of Davy' or, more formally, 'son of David'.

The first name David is found in the Bible and is of Hebrew origin. The original meaning of the name was 'darling', often used in lullabies or as a term of endearment to a child. Later, the word came to be used to mean 'friend'.

The popularity of the name David stems from Biblical times, largely as a result of the exploits of King David. Its popularity in the British Isles has been reinforced by the fact that the patron saint of Wales is St David, and two Scottish kings (in the eleventh and thirteenth centuries) bore the name. The Welsh patron saint was Archbishop of Menevia in the sixth century. His popularity accounts for the frequency of David as a Welsh first name, with its attendant nicknames Dai and Taffy. The latter is the colloquial name for a Welshman, used only by outsiders and generally with slightly derogatory connotations – as in the case of Paddy, or Limey, or Yank.

It is thus no surprise to find that the derivative surname Davies is common in Wales. (Traditionally, Davies is the

Welsh version, Davis the English.) The name is found most frequently in South Wales, as well as among the farming communities. A recent survey showed that one in twenty Welsh farming families was named Davies.

Though Davies is the most popular form of 'David's son', there are other variations. The most obvious, Davidson, while widespread, is found most frequently in Scotland and the border counties. Other variations include Davison and Davidge. Related names include Davey, Davy and Davitt (usually found in Ireland). These last, strictly speaking, are variations on the original David, also a popular surname in South Wales.

Daw, Daws and Dawson are all medieval short forms of the name Davy which it is thought was then pronounced as though spelled Dawy; while Dawkins is an affectionate pet name for the first name David.

The first name David and the surname Davies (and related names) have been widespread in England from the twelfth century, and in Scotland and Wales since even earlier times. There are references to the first name David and the surname Davy in twelfth-century records, but the first more recognisable references are to Richard Davi of Suffolk and William Davy of Oxford, both in the Hundred Rolls of 1273.

A DAVIS MISCELLANY

Davis's have the rare distinction of having a number of ingenious devices named in their honour: a double quadrant, Davis' Quadrant, invented by John Davis (Davys) (1550–1605); the Davy lamp, the first safe lamp for miners because it used gauze to separate the flame from potentially explosive gases, invented by Sir Humphry Davy (1778–1829); and the Davis Escape Apparatus, which lets submariners do just that, invented by Sir Robert Henry Davis (1870–1965).

*

The Davis Cup is the International Lawn Tennis Challenge Trophy and is competed for annually by all tennis-playing countries (rather than by individuals). It was donated in 1900 by Dwight Davis (1879–1945) who won the US doubles championship three years running – in 1899, 1900 and 1901.

*

There are no Davis-derived towns or cities in the United Kingdom and few elsewhere in the world. Canada has one town called Davis, so do 5 American states. There is a Davis Sea in the Antarctic and a Davis Island in Burma.

*

With about 343,000 namesakes Davies is the 6th most popular surname in England and Wales, while Davis accounts for another 117,000 – in combination making this name the 3rd most popular in the area. (Neither variation is common enough throughout Scotland to be counted separately.) Davies is notably popular in and around Cardiff where an estimated one in about 30 families bears the name. In descending numerical order Liverpool, Birmingham and Coventry are other Davies strongholds, while Davis is more prevalent in Bristol (one in 252 families). Around the world Davies's and Davis's are most common in Wellington (one in 220 families), Sydney (one in 283) and Canberra (one in 295). In the United States there are an estimated 1,100,000 Davis's and 39,000 Davies's, in combination making this the country's 7th most popular surname.

DOCHERTY

RELATED NAMES

Other surnames which are related as to root, derivation or usage include:

Daugherty	Dockerty	Dorrit	Dougharty
Docharty	Doherty	Dorrity	Dougherty
	O'Docherty	O'Doherty	

Docherty (or O'Docherty) is a popular Irish name which comes from the Gaelic O'Dochartargh (the prefix 'O' means 'descendant of'). O'Dochartargh is derived from the Gaelic first name Dochartach, which was originally a nickname meaning variously 'stern', 'obstructive', or 'hurtful'.

As with virtually all names transliterated from the Gaelic – where the letters are often not equivalent in sound to the corresponding letters in English – there are many variations of Docherty. The most frequent are Dougharty, Dougherty, Doherty, Docharty and Daugherty. All originate mainly from Ulster and Donegal (part of the ancient Ulster, but not of the modern province so named, being now part of the Republic), and are still found there in profusion. The name also occurs, though rarely, on the Isle of Man.

Furthermore, the form Doherty (or O'Doherty) is corruptly derived from the name O'Doorty, a Tipperary name which derives from the Gaelic O'Dubhartargh. The root here is utterly different from Dochartach and its actual meaning remains obscure, apart from the prefix 'Dubh-' which means 'black'.

Dorrity is a corrupt variation of Doherty found in Oriel. Contrary to some opinions, the name Doggett is not related. It is an Old English name whose origins are obscure – possibly deriving from an Old English diminutive for dog.

A DOCHERTY MISCELLANY

Two brothers, Reginald and Hugh Doherty, dominated turn-of-the-century English lawn tennis. Reginald, known as 'Big Do', was All-England singles champion at Wimbledon from 1897 to 1900 and was followed, from 1902 to 1906, by Hugh ('Little Do'). They were also doubles champions from 1897 to 1905, while Hugh became American national champion in 1903, the year in which the brothers jointly wrote the sports classic, *On Lawn Tennis*. Between them, the pair won 19 championships in 10 years.

*

Dora Jean Dougherty, US aviation psychologist and pilot, set two world records in 1961 for women helicopter pilots. She flew a Bell 47G-3 helicopter to an altitude of 19,406 feet. Two days later she climbed back into her machine and made a 404-mile hop in only 4 hours 26 minutes, beating the existing record by nearly 60 miles. She also claimed a third record for the point-to-point speed of the flight. All world records for women helicopter pilots had previously been held by Russians.

*

English footballer Michael Docherty is, like his famous father, Tommy, a first-rate defender. He became Burnley's youngest-ever captain when, at 19, he headed the League side against Everton on 22 November 1969.

*

The surname (and its variations) is uncommonly used as the name of towns and geographic features. There is a Dochart River in central Scotland and a small town in the United States (Georgia) called Dougherty Plain.

*

With about 9,500 namesakes Docherty is the 75th most popular surname in Scotland. Thus about one out of every 550 Scots is named Docherty. With about 22,000, the variant spelling Doherty is Ireland's 15th most popular surname. (Neither version of the surname is common enough throughout England and Wales to be counted separately.) Around the world Dochertys and Dohertys are most common in Melbourne (one in 1,925 families), Sydney (one in 2,928) and Ottawa (one in 3,170). In the United States there are fewer than 10,000 Dochertys, so an accurate count is not available for this version. There are also just under 30,000 estimated Dohertys. Thus this is their 1,068th most popular surname.

DOYLE

RELATED NAMES

Other surnames which are related as to root, derivation or usage include:

Doole Dougal D'Oyley Doyley Doylie MacDowell O'Doyle

There are two entirely separate Doyles, that which occurs more frequently being of Irish origin. Here Doyle (or O'Doyle) stems from the Irish Gaelic O'Dubhgail, which in turn comes from the first name Dubhgail. In Irish Gaelic 'Dubh' means 'black' and 'gail' means 'foreigner'. Thus Dubhgail should originally have been the name given to any dark foreigner. However, with a typically Irish twist, Dubhgail, 'dark stranger', was the name which the Irish chose to give to their blond Scandinavian invaders during Viking times. Thus many Irish Doyles were originally Vikings, of Norse origin.

The Vikings aside, this name was well established in Ireland long before the Anglo-Norman invasion. Three other well-known Irish names stem from the same non-Nordic root as Doyle. These are Dougal, Doole and MacDowell.

Doyle, Dougal, Doole and MacDowell all originate from the Gaelic word Dubhgail, yet their occurrences and history appear to be quite distinct. Doyle is one of the most popular names in Leinster, whereas Dougal is found in both Scotland and Ireland. MacDowell, on the other hand, is the Irish form of a Scottish family name which originates in the Hebrides. The MacDowells probably came to Ireland as servants of the Norse settlers. The name MacDowell is now widespread in Ulster, but in large part this is due to immigration from Scotland since Cromwellian times. These MacDowells were originally Scottish, though the origin of the name is the same.

The English name is quite distinct from the Irish name and its Celtic variations. This Doyle is a place name, stemming from the Old French de Oilgi or de Ouilli, and came to

England with William the Conqueror. The variation Doyley clearly indicates the French connection. There are no fewer than five villages called Ouilly in the Calvados region of Normandy (the place name means 'Olius's place' and contains a late Latin personal name). The English Doyles are thought to have originated from the village of Ouilli-le-Bassett in the canton of Falaise.

Several Doyle, D'Oyley variations appear in the Domesday Book for 1086. These range from de Oilgi to de Olgi and even de Oilleio.

A DOYLE MISCELLANY

The doily takes its name from a seventeenth-century shopkeeper in the Strand by the name of Doyle. He sold a popular light woollen fabric much favoured for summer wear which, by the eighteenth century, had moved to the table.

*

America has had a number of notable criminal Doyles, including Little Patsy Doyle, vicious leader of New York's nineteenth-century Hudson Dusters Club; Jess Doyle, a member of the notorious Ma Barker gang of bank robbers and kidnappers whose criminal forays, executed with military precision, netted over £1.5 million; and Dorsey Doyle, a kingpin in the Whyos Gang, whose members didn't exactly enjoy good health: over a hundred murders took place in their club house.

*

Sir Arthur Conan Doyle's Sherlock Holmes is perhaps the most enduring detective in all of fiction. Part of that fame, however, is built on sand: in none of the stories does Holmes say, 'Elementary, my dear Watson'.

*

Famed caricaturist Richard Doyle (1824–83) designed *Punch*'s original cover, which remained unchanged until the 1950s.

*

Just 5 towns in the world bear this name. New Zealand has a Doyleston while the United States has 2 Doyles, a Doylestown and a Doylesville. No significant geographic feature relates to Doyle.

*

In England, Scotland and Wales Doyle is not common enough to be counted separately. In Ireland, with about 24,000 namesakes, Doyle is the 12th most popular surname. Around the world Doyles are most common in Sydney (one in 1,584 families), Canberra (one in 1,769) and Melbourne (one in 2,226). In the United States there are an estimated 82,000 Doyles, making this their 334th most popular surname.

EDWARDS

RELATED NAMES

Other surnames which are related as to root, derivation or usage include:

Beddard   Bedward   Edkins   Edward
Edwardes   Edwardson

The name Edwards means 'dependant of Edward', as in the rarer, more specific form Edwardson. The surname and the modern first name both derive from the Old English name Eadweard, which means 'guardian of prosperity or happiness'. This name is closely related to, but quite distinct from, those other Old English names Edwin (meaning 'prosperity-friend' or 'rich friend') and Edmund (meaning 'prosperity-protector').

The first name Edward was popular in England long before the Norman Conquest, and has remained so ever since. No fewer than eight Kings of England since the Norman Conquest have been called Edward (equalled only by the Henrys). Prior to the Conquest, Edward was the name of several other English kings. Alfred the Great was succeeded by his son Edward (899–925), Edward the Martyr reigned from 975 to 979, and the last Saxon king before the unfortunate Harold was Edward the Confessor (1042–66). This last Edward also became a saint, and as such became patron saint of England until the adoption of the foreign St George.

Edward is one of the few purely English first names to have spread to the Continent, where it retains a certain popularity to this day. (Here it is usually adapted slightly, as in the French Edouard, the Scandinavian Edvard, and the Spanish Eduardo.) Edward has several popular English variations as well. Some of these have become permanently associated with other fields. Ned has been a widespread variant of Edward since the fourteenth century, and Neddy is now the popular name for a donkey. Ted and Teddy are also well known. Ed and Eddie are more modern variants, sometimes deriving from Edmund or Edwin, though the surname Eddy is quite distinct from the surname Edwards. It derives from the Old English Eadwig meaning 'prosperity war'. Bedward and Beddard are Welsh variants from 'ab Edward', 'son of Edward'.

There are numerous references to Edwards in the 1066 Domesday Book – in the form of Eaduuardus, Aeduuardus, Eduuard(us). (These variations show that the letter 'w' in Edward literally originated as a 'double u' – neatly illuminating the origins of that letter.) However, by 1219 we can see the name used in its present spelling – when one William Edward appears in the Curia Regis Rolls for Suffolk.

AN EDWARDS MISCELLANY

The most Noble Order of the Garter was founded by Edward III in 1348. Members of the Order have included the Duke of Wellington and Winston Churchill.

*

The American clergyman Jonathan Edwards (1703–58) was renowned for his gift as a preacher. Unfortunately, such was the powerful effect of his oratory, that when he led a religious revival in 1734 he drove many of his converts to suicide. After this, he became president of the college which later became Princeton University.

*

Michael Edwardes, chairman of much troubled BL (formerly British Leyland), was born in South Africa. His meteoric rise in the commercial world came to public notice after he won the *Guardian* Young Businessman's Award. His appointment as chairman of BL has made him a popular target for union leaders, and his efforts to save the ailing British car industry – notably by linking it with the Japanese firm of Honda – have frequently raised storms of controversy.

*

The Fleet Street editorship record is held by Robert Edwards who served four terms as editor of a national newspaper: *Daily Express* (1961 and again in 1963), *Sunday People* (1966) and *Sunday Mirror* (1972).

*

The United Kingdom has one related-name town – Edwardstone, while Australia has an Edwardstown and New Zealand an Edwardson. The United States has 7 Edwards-related towns.

*

With about 179,000 namesakes Edwards is the 20th most popular surname in England and Wales. (The name is not common enough throughout Scotland to be counted separately.) Edwards is notably popular in and around Cardiff where an estimated one in about 130 families bears the name. In descending numerical order Liverpool, Birmingham and Bristol are other Edwards strongholds. Around the world Edwards's are most common in Canberra (one in 479 families), Melbourne (one in 619) and Auckland (one in 678). The United States has more Edwards's than the entire population of Nottingham – an estimated total of just over 313,000 makes this their 50th most popular surname.

EVANS

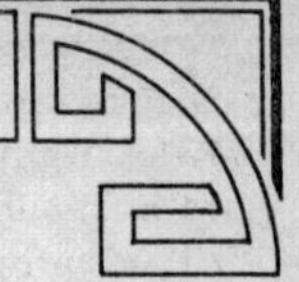

RELATED NAMES

Other surnames which are related as to root, derivation or usage include:

Beavan	Bevans	Evanson	Heaven
Beavon	Bevens	Evanston	Heavens
Beevens	Evan	Evens	Hevens
Bevan	Evance	Evins	Jones (see also)

The surname Evans derives from the first name Evan, or Ewan. The suffix '-s' means 'dependant of'; so Evans means 'son or dependant of Evan'. Evan, or Ewan, is the Welsh name for John and was originally Ioan, which is now more common in Wales in the form of Iean (pronounced Yian, to rhyme with 'iron'). Ewan is now more common as a Scots first name, deriving from the original John by way of Scots Gaelic.

It is also possible that some examples of the widespread and historic Welsh name Owen could be derived from variants of this source (it usually represents a quite separate tradition). Indisputably certain is the fact that the Welsh name Jones (i.e. 'son of John – Johnson – Jones') is equivalent to Evans. Thus two of the most common Welsh names, Jones and Evans, originate from the name John.

The first name John originates from the Hebrew Jochanaan, which means 'God is gracious'. The Latin form of this name was Johannes, and in this form it was brought back to Central Europe by the Crusaders. Here it became popular in many countries, each forming their own variation. Thus John is Johan or Hans in Germany, and Jean in France. The name was largely popular because of its Biblical use – with John the Baptist, and St John the Divine, author of the Book of Revelations.

In rare instances the surname Evan(s) represents a substitute for Owen(s) derived from the Latin first name

Eugenius (now found in the form Eugene). Eugenius originally meant 'high-born'.

There are many variations of the surname Evans – the most common being Evens, Evins, Heaven, Heavens, Evance and Evanson.

The earliest references in the records to the name Evans came in the 1568 Subsidy Rolls. Here the Rolls for Suffolk list one John Evans. This reference is late compared with most other popular names, because the name Evans only evolved as such about the year 1500.

AN EVANS MISCELLANY

The Welsh archaeologist, Sir Arthur Evans (1851–1941), is famed for his excavations at Knossos on Crete which uncovered the Minoan civilisation. This provided the vital missing link between Ancient Egypt and the rise of Ancient Greece.

*

The Evanses are physical achievers. The Olympic record for 400 metres of 43.86 seconds has stood since 1968 and was achieved by Lee Edward Evans of the US. On the other hand, the world record for high kicks has stood since 1939 at 8,005 kicks in 4 hours 40 minutes. It was set by Veronica Evans at the old Pathétone Studios in Wardour Street, London.

*

The Evans Cup is the name of the Major Public Schools squash competition.

*

Edward Evans was one of the unfortunate victims of the notorious 'Moors Murderers' (1963–5), Ian Brady and Myra Hindley; while Timothy John Evans was hanged in 1950 for his wife's murder. The latter lived at 10 Rillington Place with mass-murderer and necrophiliac, John Christie. Later Christie was arrested and charged with Mrs Evans' murder together with over a dozen others, mostly of prostitutes. Controversy still ranges as to whether Evans was in fact hanged as an innocent man. The case had much to do with the abolition of capital punishment in the UK.

*

There are towns called Evanton and Evans Mead in the United Kingdom. Australia and New Zealand have Evansdales while Canada has an Evansburg and an Evansville. This latter town name is common in the United States where there are 6 out of a total of 13 Evans-related towns and cities. Bermuda and New Zealand have Evans Bays.

*

With about 276,000 namesakes Evans is the 7th most popular surname in England and Wales. (The name is not common enough throughout Scotland to be counted separately.) Evans is notably popular in and around Cardiff where an estimated one in about 50 families bears the name. In descending numerical order Birmingham, Liverpool and Coventry are other Evans strongholds. Around the world Evans's are most common in Canberra (one in 535 families), Wellington (one in 553) and Sydney (one in 574). The United States has more Evans's than the entire population of Newcastle – an estimated total of just under 361,000 makes this their 45th most popular surname.

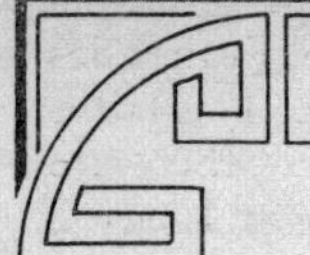

GALLAGHER

RELATED NAMES

Other surnames which are related as to root, derivation or usage include:

Galbraith	Gallacher	Galle	Gaul
Gall	Gallaher	Galsworthy	Gaw

O'Gallagher

The surname Gallagher is of Irish origin. The Irish Gaelic form of Gallagher (or O'Gallagher) is O'Gallichobhair, and derives from the Gaelic word 'gallchobhar', which means 'foreign help'. This has a similar root to the Scots name Galbraith, which comes from the Scots Gaelic meaning 'foreign Briton' (which usually refers to early Welsh settlers in Scotland), and to the English name Gall (or Gaul) which is of Breton Gaelic origin and means simply 'foreigner'.

The name Gallagher came mainly from Donegal and the eastern Ulster borderlands, where it was often one of the main family clans.

The name is highly popular in Ireland and is also amongst the top sixty names in Scotland. The Scottish popularity is due entirely to Irish immigration and does not stem from any native Gaelic derivation.

The name has been popular and widespread in Ireland since the fifteenth century. However, there are no references to this name in any early English records or rolls. The presumed reason for this is because the name did not appear in England in large numbers, or with its holder having sufficient status, until the major immigrations during the nineteenth century.

Because Gaelic and English do not run parallel in a strictly literal sense, the transliteration of the original O'Gallichobhair into English has resulted in a wide variety of different spellings. This is frequently the case with Gaelic names, though the twenty-three variants of Gallagher would seem to be exceptional. The main variations in the anglicised

Gallagher are Gallacher and Gallaher, though some variations even begin with 'Gol-'.

A GALLAGHER MISCELLANY

Saint Gall (c.550–645) and twelve disciples established a monastery at the source of the Steinach from which the famous monastery, present Swiss town and canton all take their names.

*

'Gallagher's Frolics' is a traditional Irish jig.

*

The Gallaher Ulster Golf Championship is sponsored by the cigarette firm. For professionals and selected amateurs, this stroke-play tourney is played every August at the Shandon Park course outside Belfast. The prize money is over £4,000, making it Ulster's major golfing event.

*

The cooperative retail movement in Ireland was founded by one Patrick Gallagher (1873–1964).

*

There are no towns, cities or major geographic features which are Gallagher-related.

*

In England, Scotland and Wales Gallagher is not common enough to be counted separately. In Ireland with about 23,000 namesakes Gallagher is the 14th most popular surname. Around the world Gallaghers are most common in Canberra (one in 1,045 families), Sydney (one in 2,541) and Auckland (one in 3,091). In the United States there are an estimated 77,000 Gallaghers. This makes it the country's 362nd most popular surname.

GREEN

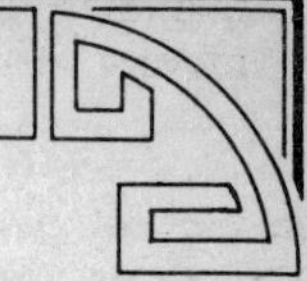

RELATED NAMES

Other surnames which are related as to root, derivation or usage include:

Greenacre	Greenhalf	Greenist	Greenwell
Greenall	Greenhalgh	Greenleaf	Greenwood
Greenaway	Greenhall	Greenlees	Grene
Greenbank	Greenham	Greenley	Grenfell
Greenberry	Greenhead	Greenman	Grenville
Greenburgh	Greenhill	Greenough	Grindlay
Greenbury	Greenhoff	Greenshields	Grindley
Greene	Greenhouse	Greenslade	Grinham
Greener	Greenhow	Greensmith	Grinley
Greenfield	Greenhowe	Greensted	Grinnell
Greenford	Greenidge	Greenstreet	Grinstead
Greengrass	Greening	Greenway	Grinsted

The name Green stems from the Old English word 'grene', which means village green. Originally this was part of the common land where the villagers all had certain free grazing rights. Green is one of the oldest names in England, for obvious reasons in a country which was once such a 'green and pleasant land'. In this short form the name meant 'one who lives near the village green'.

There is, however, another derivation of Green. Since very early times the word green has meant young, fresh, immature or callow. Often a villager would be called 'green' because of something he had done in his youth; the nickname would stick and in time it would become the family name. Despite this, Green has long been a popular English name. In 1853 Green was the seventeenth most popular name in England. Now it has crept up to sixteenth.

Some of today's Greens (or Greenes or Grenes) are shortened versions of 'attegreen' -- at the green. The word green enters into many place names which have given rise to surnames, and these each have their own different meanings, many not so obvious as they would appear.

Most Greenfields, for instance, derive not from 'green fields', but from Grenville, a place name in France and the name of several Anglo-Norman families. Many Jews who fled from the pogroms of Eastern Europe during the final decades of the last century decided to take English names when they reached the safety of these shores. Some simply chose any English name which took their fancy. Others adopted the name of the place where they had landed in England; there are, for instance, several Jewish families called Hastings. (As Michael Hastings, the Jewish writer, remarked, he was lucky his family didn't arrive at Dungeness or Wapping.) Other Jews anglicised their original names so that, for example, German-Jewish Grunwalds might become Greenwoods.

Some Greenfields derive from an earlier anglicisation. Several of William the Conqueror's men who crossed to fight at the Battle of Hastings came from the tiny Normandy village of Grainville-la-Teinturiere (which is now in the Seine-Maritime department). When they settled in England their name was quickly corrupted to Grenville (or even Grenfell), and later became Greenfield. These, and other, apparently far-fetched changes are easier to understand when you realise that in those times there was no standardised spelling in English. People even spelt their own name in several different ways. As late as the sixteenth century we find as many as thirteen different variations in the spelling of the name Shakespeare, many deriving from Shakespeare's own casual usage.

Another related surname is Greenford. This literally means 'ford at a green', but where the name is concerned it derives from a particular place, the small town just west of London in Middlesex. Greenhalgh, another common name, means 'green place' (especially the Lancashire examples), and Greenacre means 'green field' (not necessarily a strict acre). This latter name is thought to have originated from Norfolk.

Greenham sometimes meant 'green river meadow', while this name also originates from the places of the same name in Berkshire and Somerset, though the Greenham in Somerset may be a corruption of 'grind', describing a millstream. Greenhowe and Greenhoff mean 'green mount or hill' and mainly originated (with many variations of spelling) in north and west Yorkshire.

Greensmiths, on the other hand, were originally coppersmiths. The reason they were called 'green' was because the flames of their fires would turn green as they worked their copper, or, according to some, because copper acquires a green patina as it is worked.

The earliest Green in the records is Geoffrey de Grene, who appears in the 1188 Pipe Rolls for Kent.

A GREEN MISCELLANY

A Green was making aviation history before the Wright brothers were born. Balloonist extraordinary Charles Green (1793–1841) astonished the world by flying from Vauxhall Gardens, London, to Weilberg, Germany (480 miles), in just under 18 hours (1836). In all, he made 527 ascents, including one which exceeded 27,000 feet in height.

*

The popular English melody 'Greensleeves' is of Elizabethan origin (published 1581) and is mentioned in Shakespeare. It was initially described as 'a new courtly sonnet of the Lady Greensleeves'.

*

George Green (1793–1841) is widely regarded as the father of modern physics in Great Britain. He was the first to attempt, to apply mathematical formulae to electricity and magnetism. 'Green's Theorem' is named after his work.

*

Baron William Wyndham Grenville (1759–1834), as Prime Minister, abolished Britain's overseas slave trade on his last day in office.

*

A man bearing a Green-related surname caused the American Revolution: politician George Grenville (1712–70) initiated the tax acts which caused the colonies to revolt.

*

The 'Green Man' is now a common name for a pub. The origins of the name go back to pre-Christian times and are thought to be connected with fertility cults. The image of the Green Man is found on some thirteenth- to fifteenth-century churches in connection with the Easter resurrection.

*

David Green (1886–1973) is better known by his pseudonym, David Ben-Gurion, Israeli statesman and first Premier of his country.

*

One Edward W. Green committed the first bank robbery in American history, in 1863. He was caught within 24 hours.

*

Richard Grenville (1542–91) is one of Britain's greatest naval heroes. Separated from his own fleet, his ship *The Revenge* took on 15 Spanish men-of-war and fought them for over 12 hours. Finally Grenville was captured and died of his wounds. His exploit is celebrated in Tennyson's poem 'The Revenge' and in Charles Kingsley's novel *Westward Ho!*.

*

A total of 109 towns and cities contain the word green. The United Kingdom alone accounts for 42 of these, ranging from Green Bank to Greenthorpe. This includes no fewer than 5 Greenfields. The United States has 9 towns and cities with this latter name, as well as 6 Greensboros and 5 Greensburgs.

Given its descriptive nature, countless rivers, lakes, mountains and islands bear the name; so does a country – Greenland.

*

With about 185,000 namesakes Green is the 16th most popular surname in England and Wales. (The name is not common enough throughout Scotland to be counted separately.) Green is notably popular in and around Sheffield where an estimated one in about 210 families bears the name. In descending numerical order Birmingham, Leicester and Nottingham are other Green strongholds. Around the world Greens are most common in Auckland (one in 525 families), Sydney (one in 573) and Wellington (one in 723). The United States has more Greens than the entire population of Bristol – an estimated total of just over 427,000 makes this their 37th most popular surname.

GRIFFITHS

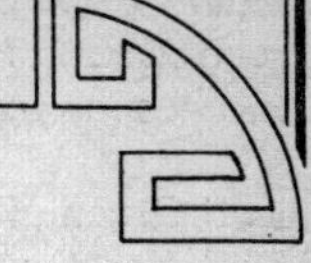

RELATED NAMES

Other surnames which are related as to root, derivation or usage include:

Griffen Griffin Griffis Griffith

The surname Griffith (whence Griffiths) derives from the Old Welsh Griphiud. The suffix '-iud' means 'lord', though the meaning of the stem remains debatable. One plausible explanation is that it derives from the common Latin appellation Rufus, which means 'red-haired', though there is no proof as to this root.

Griffin is a pet-name form of Griffith which is popular in Wales; this was the name given to many early Welsh princes. Griffin is also the name given to a Welsh heraldic dragon seen on the Welsh national flag, as well as on many Welsh pub signs. The pub-sign griffin is normally green, though on the flag it is red on a half-green, half-white horizontal background.

However, the name Griffin is not always Welsh (whereas the name Griffith is). It originates from two distinct areas – the Welsh border country and the eastern counties of England. The eastern Griffins are of Breton origin, coming to England after the Battle of Hastings.

The earliest reference to the name Griffin is in the Calendarium Genealogicum during the reign of Edward I, where one Tuder fil Griffini is mentioned. (The 'fil' is short for the Latin filius, meaning 'son of', the consequent name being Latinised from the doubtless spoken form of Griffin to Griffinus.)

The earliest reference to the name Griffiths is found in the Wills at Chester for the year 1585. Here one John Ap-Griffith is recorded. ('Ap' or 'ab' is Welsh for 'son of' – as in John ab Evan, which became corrupted to the name Bevan.) The root name Griffith gave rise to the variants Griffiths and Griffis. Both of these mean 'dependant of Griffith', the suffix '-s' meaning 'dependant of' or 'son of' (compare the name Bennett, which gives Bennettson and Bennetts).

A GRIFFITHS MISCELLANY

In Elizabethan times Sir Henry Griffith's daughter, Ann, devoted all her love and energies to their Yorkshire mansion, Burton Agnes Hall. One evening, while returning from a visit, she was set upon by robbers and savagely beaten. Before she died she begged her family to let her head remain within the walls of her beloved house. She threatened to make the house unliveable if they failed to honour her wish, and promptly proceeded to do so when the family, believing her injuries had deranged her mind, buried her in the family vault. Moans, loud crashing noises and the sound of slammed doors filled the house and strange personal disasters befell the inhabitants until the skull was disinterred and brought inside. Today it is firmly ensconced behind a massive screen in the central hall.

*

In March 1925, one of America's most violent tornados hit Griffin, Indiana. It destroyed 196 out of the 200 buildings in the town and left 50 dead in its wake.

*

The first of the great clipper ships such as the *Cutty Sark* was the *Rainbow*, designed by the American naval architect, John Willis Griffiths (1809–82).

*

D.W. Griffith (1874–1948) is regarded by many as the father of the film industry. In search of sun he moved his studio to a sleepy town called Hollywood.

*

Griffiths are champions. The American professional boxer Emile Griffiths (b.1938) has won five world titles, while Terry Griffiths (b.1947) won the world's snooker championship in 1979.

*

This name is relatively rarely incorporated in towns and geographic features. In the United Kingdom there are towns called Griff and Griffithstown, the United States has a Griffithville and a Griffin while Australia has a Griffith, which is also the name of a Canadian island.

*

With about 117,000 namesakes Griffiths is the 47th most

popular surname in England and Wales. (The name is not common enough throughout Scotland to be counted separately.) Griffiths is notably popular in and around Cardiff where an estimated one in about 130 families bears the name. In descending numerical order Liverpool, Birmingham and Bristol are other Griffiths strongholds. Around the world Griffiths's are most common in Canberra (one in 767 families), Auckland (one in 869) and Sydney (one in 1,020). The United States has more Griffiths's than the entire population of Doncaster – an estimated total of just over 309,000 makes this their 54th most popular surname.

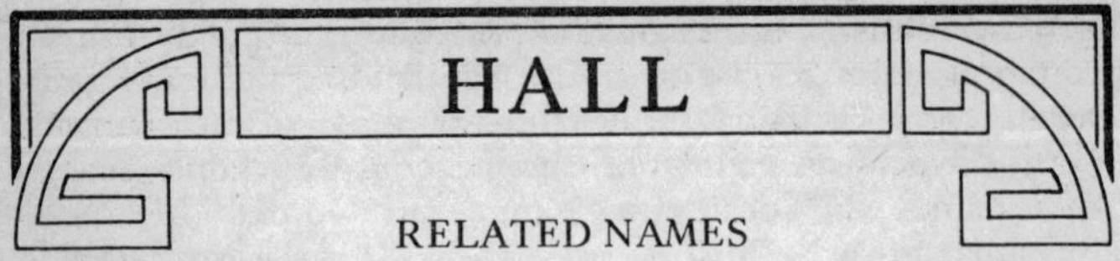

HALL

RELATED NAMES

Other surnames which are related as to root, derivation or usage include:

Alstead	Hallé	Halline	Halman
Hailey	Haller	Hallman	Halsted
Hallam	Halley	Halls	Halston
Halle	Hallfield	Hallstead	Halstone

The surname Hall is a local name from the Old English Hall or Heall, meaning 'a hall or large house'. The name Hall was originally given to someone who lived in or by (or was employed at) the hall or manor. Field, Castle and Stone are other common examples of local names of this type.

However, not all Halls derive from this source. This name frequently occurs in the north-east of England, and it seems that here the name Hall is a local name deriving from the Old Norse for a 'boulder or slope' and was given to someone who lived on, near, or under some prominent boulder or hillside. (As such, it would mean much the same as the name Stone.)

A variation of this latter derivation is the name Hallam, which is found mainly in nearby West Yorkshire. Here, Hallam is a local name deriving from the Old Norse for 'at the stone or slope'. However, in some cases the name Hallam was given to a native of Hallam in the old parish of Sheffield.

The surname Hall goes back to early feudal times. One Warin de Halla is mentioned in the 1178 Pipe Rolls for Essex, and two examples of the name appear in the Hundred Rolls of 1273. Here one Roger de la Halle is recorded in the Cambridgeshire records, while a Walter de la Halle appears in the records for Salop. (The Norman French 'de la' would suggest that in these cases they were probably employed at the hall or manor.)

A HALL MISCELLANY

Halley's Comet, named for Edward Halley (1656–1742) and

first observed by him in 1682, is probably the brightest and most spectacular known to us. Its brilliant passage across the heavens has long been thought to presage great historical events. It was seen in 1066 at the time of the Norman Conquest and is next due in 1986.

*

Big Ben, actually the name of the bell, not the clock, is named after the rotund parliamentarian Sir Benjamin Hall (1802–67), who was Minister of Works when the bell was cast for St Stephen's Tower.

*

Aluminium was made practicable by the invention of the electrolysis process by the American chemist, Charles Martin Hall (1863–1914).

*

The United Kingdom has 21 Hall-related towns and cities. These range from Halland to Hall Thwaites. Canada has 4 towns with Hall-related names while the United States has 14. Related town names are prevalent throughout Europe, there being 32 in all. These range from Austria's Hall to Denmark's Hallundback. Hall is unusually common as a geographic name ranging from the United Kingdom's Halley Bay to Hall Table Mountain in Mozambique.

*

With about 181,000 namesakes Hall is the 17th most popular surname in England and Wales. (The name is not common enough throughout Scotland to be counted separately.) Hall is notably popular in and around Teesside where an estimated one in about 200 families bears the name. In descending numerical order Leicester, Sheffield and Leeds are other Hall strongholds. Around the world Halls are most common in Melbourne (one in 582 families), Canberra (one in 590) and Sydney (one in 601). The United States has more Halls than the entire population of Bristol – an estimated total of just over 494,000 makes this their 24th most popular surname.

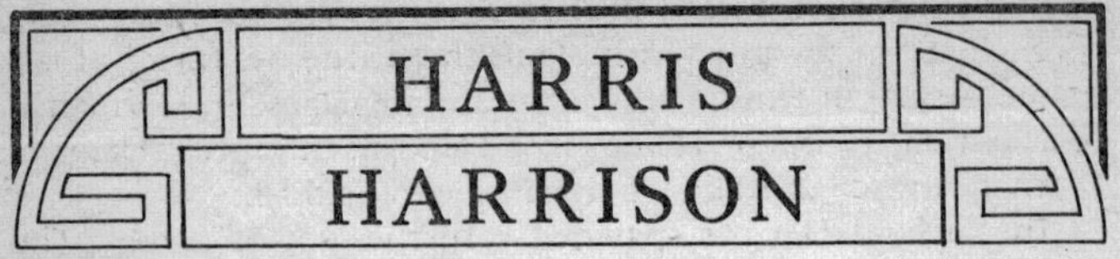

RELATED NAMES

Other surnames which are related as to root, derivation or usage include:

Harison	Harriot	Harry	Henry
Harrey	Harriott	Henderson	Heriot
Harrie	Harriss	Hendry	Herriot
Harries	Harrisson	Henrieson	Herry

Herryson

The name Harris is an English derivative of the colloquial pronunciations of the name Henry (Herry and Harry). All the English kings we now call Henry were known in their time as King Harry. The first King Henry (or Harry) was the first Norman king to be born on English soil. This fact encouraged his popularity, and in turn made the name itself popular. Between the eleventh and sixteenth centuries there were eight English kings so named – a number equalled only by the Edwards. Amongst these were three of England's greatest kings: King Henry V who won the Battle of Agincourt and is now immortalised in Shakespeare's play; King Henry VIII with his six wives and decisive ways with matrimonial disputes; and the less spectacular Henry VII whose long and prosperous reign laid the foundations for the glories of Henry VIII and then the Elizabethan age. Before Henry I there were just five Henrys listed as tenants in the Domesday Book, but after his reign the name quickly grew in popularity, becoming amongst the dozen most popular English first names.

The origins of the name Henry go back to Old German. Here the name Heimirick first appeared. This was a compound of the word 'haimi', meaning 'house' or 'home', and 'ric', meaning 'ruler'. With the coming of the Romans, the name Haimiric became Latinised to Henricus. Post-

Roman migration spread the name which evolved into Italian, French, Spanish, and so on. Thus there are now forms of the name Henry in almost all European languages. In German it is Heinrich, Heinz or Heine. It is Hendrik in Dutch, Henri in French, Enrico in Italian and Enrique in Spanish.

In England Harris's spawned a further set of names. The best known of these are Harrison, Henderson and Hendry. The rarer name Harrissmith is not derived from Harris, but is almost certainly a corruption of Arrowsmith, a maker of arrowheads.

Of the many surnames derived from the original Henry (or Harry), Harris and Harrison are by far the most popular, both names appearing all over England and Wales. However, each has its prevalent areas. In the south of England, below a line drawn between Lincoln and Chester, you are more likely to come across the name Harris. It is most frequent in Gwent and South Wales as well as in the South Midlands, especially Worcestershire, Warwickshire, Oxford and Northampton. It is also fairly popular down in Devon and Cornwall. Inexplicably, it is less frequent in the eastern part of England.

Harrisons, on the other hand, are mostly found in the north, appearing most frequently in Cumbria, Lancashire and Yorkshire. Recent evidence seems to suggest that the Harrisons are on the march south and large numbers have been noted in Derbyshire and Nottinghamshire, with concentrated outposts as far south as the English Channel coast. Indeed, if present trends continue in the war between Harris's and Harrisons, the outcome is inevitable: Harrison domination throughout the land.

Harris was also a very popular name with the Jews who fled to England in the last decades of the nineteenth century to escape Russian and Polish pogroms. Their Eastern European names were often unpronounceable to the English and made their owners feel socially conspicuous. Consequently, they often adopted solid English names; many chose Harris.

A great many of these immigrants were in the garment trade, but the famous Scottish Harris tweed has nothing to do with either the Jewish Harris's or the English ones. This tweed cloth is named after the Hebridean Island of Harris where the cloth is woven.

One of the earliest references to the name is to one John Herryson mentioned in a charter dating from 1376.

A HARRIS MISCELLANY

The Harrison Cup is one of the main events in the polo calendar and takes place at Cowdray Park each July.

*

There have been two Presidents of the United States called Harrison (the 9th and the 23rd), a distinction shared only by the Johnsons and the Roosevelts.

*

The Harris Movement takes its name from the founding prophet, William Wade Harris (1858–1929). It is the largest mass movement for conversion to Christianity in West Africa, while another major movement is also Harris-connected. Chicago lawyer Paul Harris (1868–1947) founded the worldwide Rotary Club in 1905.

*

The first true English encyclopaedia, the *Dictionary of Arts and Sciences* (1704), was edited by John Harris (c. 1666–1719).

*

Britain's most successful arsonist, Leopold Harris (b.1894) caused the Great Arson Scandal of 1933 which revealed that insurance-company employees and members of the Fire Brigade had helped to defraud the insurers of hundreds of thousands of pounds annually for years.

*

The entertainment world abounds with stars with the surname: Kathleen Harrison (b. 1898), Julie Harris (b. 1925), Rosemary Harris (b. 1930), Phil Harris (b. 1906), Rex Harrison (b. 1908), Richard Harris (b. 1932) and Rolf Harris (b. 1930).

*

The Harrisburg, Pennsylvania, flood was at the heart of America's 1972 Hurricane Agnes disaster. In the town and the surrounding area 122 lives were lost, with over £2 billion in damage.

*

The United Kingdom has towns named Harris and Harrishead.

There are also Harristowns in Canada and the US which has 2 out of a total of 23 Harris-related cities and towns. Mountains, lakes, rivers and islands around the world bear the name as does a forest in the United Kingdom.

*

With about 165,000 namesakes Harris is the 25th most popular surname in England and Wales while Harrison accounts for another 144,000 – in combination making the name the 7th most popular in the area. (Neither name is common enough throughout Scotland to be counted separately.) Harris is notably popular in and around Cardiff where an estimated one in about 175 families bears the name while Harrison is most popular in Teesside (an estimated one in 245 families). Around the world Harris's and Harrisons are most common in Wellington (one in 370 families), Auckland (one in 525) and Sydney (one in 712). In the United States the two names are tallied together and account for 729,000 people, a larger number than the total population of Leeds. In combination this makes it the country's 11th most popular surname.

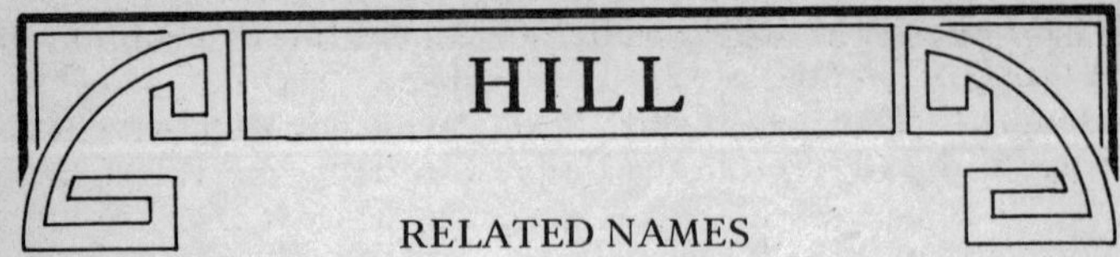

HILL

RELATED NAMES

Other surnames which are related as to root, derivation or usage include:

Greenhill	Hillas	Hillhouse	Hillis
Hellman	Hille	Hilling	Hillman
Hilhouse	Hillers	Hillings	Hills
	Hilman		Hilton

The surname Hill is a local name derived from what is believed to be the Old English word 'hyll'. The name originally meant 'he who dwells at, by, or on the hill'. The reasons for its popularity are self-evident, in much the same way as other local names from medieval village life – such as Green, Hall and Ford.

There are, however, two other rare derivations of Hill. In one case it is a pet name derived from the first names of German origin beginning with Hild- (as in Hildegard), where the prefix 'Hild-' means 'battle'. In very rare cases Hill is an abbreviation of the first name Hilary, which came from the Latin and means 'cheerful'. (We get the word 'hilarious' from the same root.) In former times, Hilary was more popular as a male first name.

The name Hill is mentioned in records as far back as the 1191 Pipe Rolls for Norfolk, where one Gilbert del Hill is mentioned. 'Del' here is not Spanish or Italian, but a corruption of the Norman French 'de la', meaning 'of the', as in Walter de la Hille whose name occurs in the 1273 Hundred Rolls.

As usual, there are a number of variations on this simple local name. Hillhouse (which corrupts to Hillis and Hillers and Hillas) means 'dweller at the house on the hill'. Hilling seems to represent an Old English word 'hylling', 'hill-dweller', though Hillman can derive from two sources. It can either mean the obvious 'dweller by the slope', or it can mean 'servant of Hild' (who would originally have been

'Hild's man'). The widespread Hellman is also a corruption of this last name.

Several other names which seem to contain Hill are not derived from it. The most widespread of these are Hilliar (a form of Helliar, an occupational name, which derives from the Old English for a slater or tiler), and Hilliard (a form of Hildyard, from the Old German personal name Hildigard).

A HILL MISCELLANY

The green belts which surround most major British cities are the direct descendants of the 'open spaces' created by pioneering social and housing reformer, Octavia Hill (1838–1912), who was convinced that escape from overcrowding reduced crime and poverty.

*

Two Hills have been notable Grand Prix drivers: Phil Hill (b. 1927), the first American to win the World Championship (1961), and Graham Hill (1929–75) who took the Indianapolis 500 in his first attempt (1961), won Le Mans in 1962 as well as the Grand Prix Championship; he won the latter again in 1968. Shortly after retiring he died in a plane crash.

*

Sir Rowland Hill (1795–1879) reorganised the postal system and introduced the penny post (1840), the precursor of all modern postal systems. His first stamp, the famous 'Penny Black' with its 'bun' outline of Queen Victoria's head, is now a collectors' item (an uncancelled specimen in prime condition costs over £2,000). These stamps established a precedent still in force: Britain's name never appears on her stamps. Later, as Chairman of the London and Brighton Railway, Sir Rowland pioneered both express train service and special excursion fares.

*

Henry Hill (1809–81), one of Britain's all-time great punters, also owned an exceptionally successful stable. He won the Derby in 1846, the Two Thousand Guineas in 1850 and the Goodwood Cup in 1856 – all races he had bet on heavily: he needed the winnings to offset his heavy losses on the Stock Exchange (£40,000 in one year alone).

*

Hill's Equation in physiology is a mathematical formula for the shortening of skeletal muscle when load is increased.

*

The first Hillman car, then called Hillman-Coatelen, was built in 1907.

*

Americans Patty and Mildred Hill wrote one of the world's most popular songs, 'Happy Birthday to You' (1896). Not wishing to capitalise on this happy tune, it was not copyrighted until 1936. All royalties go to charity.

*

Sir Rowland Hill was Lord Mayor of London in 1549.

*

Largely due to its descriptive nature, Hill is remarkably prevalent both as the name of towns and cities and as a geographical name. The United Kingdom has 38 towns and cities whose names are related, including 4 Hillheads and 3 Hillsides. The number of related towns and cities elsewhere include 7 in Canada, 3 in Australia, 2 in New Zealand, 3 in South Africa and 42 in the United States (including an impressive 14 Hillsboros).

*

With about 150,000 namesakes Hill is the 30th most popular surname in England and Wales. (The name is not common enough throughout Scotland to be counted separately.) Hill is notably popular in and around Leicester where an estimated one in about 270 families bears the name. In descending numerical order Birmingham, Nottingham and Sheffield are other Hill strongholds. Around the world Hills are most common in Canberra (one in 590 families), Sydney (one in 618) and Melbourne (one in 663). The United States has more Hills than the entire population of Coventry – an estimated total of just under 435,000 makes this their 32nd most popular surname.

HUGHES

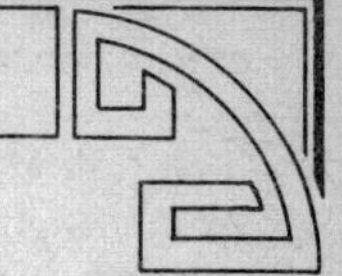

RELATED NAMES

Other surnames which are related as to root, derivation or usage include:

FitzHugh	Hews	Huckin	Huggon
FitzHughes	Hewson	Hudd	Huggons
Haw	Hooson	Hudsmith	Hugh
Hew	Hoosun	Hudson	Hughson
Hewe	How	Hue	Huglin
Hewes	Howe	Huetson	Hugo
Hewett	Howes	Huett	Hugon
Hewitt	Howkins	Huggell	Hullot
Hewlett	Howlett	Huggett	Huson
Hewlin	Hows	Huggins	Huws
MacHugh	Pugh	Pughes	

The surname Hughes derives from the first name Hugh and means 'dependant of Hugh'.

The first name Hugh is of Old German origin and comes originally from the first name Hugo, which means 'heart or mind'. The name Hugo also appears in Latin (almost certainly from the same source) where it became corrupted to Hewe and Howe. Both of these names, as well as Hugo, now appear as variant surnames.

The variants Hew, Hewes, Hews and Hewson often come from a different root – the Middle English word 'hewe' meaning 'maidservant'.

The surname Hughes is found all over England, Scotland, Wales and Ireland, though it appears in its greatest concentrations in North Wales. Here it may well have Gaelic origins, as does the name when it occurs in those parts of Scotland and Ireland that have remained relatively free from English influence. In these cases, Hughes is descended from the Irish Gaelic first name Aodh and the Scottish Gaelic names Eoghann (in Argyllshire) and Uisdeann (in the remote north-west). In Ireland the names Hugh and MacHugh (son of

Hugh) are the equivalent of the Scottish name MacKay. In Wales the name Hughes has sometimes become Pugh, Hew, or Haw.

All in all, there are nearly one hundred variations of the surname Hughes in present use. These include the first syllable varying from 'Hew-' to 'Huw-' to 'Hu-', and suffixes ranging from '-son', '-kin' and '-man' through to '-in', '-on', '-et' and '-ot'. Many of these variations stem from the widespread popularity of the first name Hugo after the Norman Conquest. As such, the name appears in the 1066 Domesday Book records for Huntingdonshire and Suffolk, though by 1084 in the Geld Roll (part of the Domesday Book) the name appeared more recognisably as Willelmus filius Hugonis. The name achieved further popularity through St Hugh of Avalon, who was Prior of Witham and Bishop of Lincoln at the turn of the thirteenth century.

The common pet form of Hugh was Hud, hence the surnames Hudd, Hudson and Hudsmith (from Hudsmough, 'Hugh's brother-in-law').

A HUGHES MISCELLANY

British showman Edwin Hughes (1813–67) originated the word 'circus' in its entertainment sense, with 'Hughes' Great Mammoth Equestrian Circus', which pioneered the use of wild animals, such as elephants, in harness.

*

'John Hughes won't save you' was a derisory World War I expression applied to prospective British draftees. Hughes, a greengrocer, was tried and convicted for concocting a scheme to save men from serving in the army.

*

Tom Brown's School Days was written by Thomas Hughes (1822–96) as an affectionate tribute to his own Rugby school days.

*

All those who wear hearing aids are indebted to British professor David Edward Hughes (1831–1900) whose experiments in the transmission properties of carbon fibres were critical to the development of the hearing aid as well as to that of microphones. He also invented the earliest telegraphic teleprinter. His very substantial fortune was bequeathed to London hospitals.

*

American Peter Cooper Hewitt (1861–1921) invented the mercury vapour lamp and a remarkable early version of the helicopter (1918).

*

Noted English navigator and explorer Henry Hudson (d.1611) reached America on his third attempt to find the legendary Northwest Passage to the Orient. After cruising off Newfoundland he explored the coast of what is now New England, then proceeded as far south as Delaware Bay. Along the way he discovered the New York river that now bears his name. A fourth voyage took him to what is now Hudson's Bay where his ship was frozen in, the crew rebelled and he was set adrift. It is probable he perished in his namesake.

*

There are no name-related towns or major geographic features in the United Kingdom. Australia has a town called Hughes, and there are 2 such towns in the United States as well as a Hughes Springs and a Hughesville. Canada has a Hughes river in Manitoba.

*

With about 176,000 namesakes Hughes is the 21st most popular surname in England and Wales. There are over 9,000 Hughes's in Scotland where it is 76th in popularity, while in Ireland an estimated 16,000 Hughes's makes it the 34th most popular surname there. Hughes is notably popular in and around Liverpool where an estimated one in about 135 families bears the name. In descending numerical order Cardiff, Birmingham and Manchester are other Hughes strongholds. Around the world Hughes's are most common in Canberra (one in 676 families), Auckland (one in 944) and Wellington (one in 949). The United States has more Hughes's than the entire population of Derby – an estimated total of just over 243,000 makes this their 76th most popular surname.

JACKSON

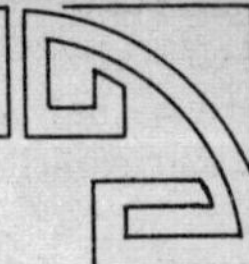

RELATED NAMES

Other surnames which are related as to root, derivation or usage include:

Jack	Jacketts	Jacks	Jaggar
Jackalin	Jacking	Jacot	Jaggard
Jackaman	Jacklin	Jacson	Jagger
Jackard	Jackling	Jager	Jaggs
Jackett	Jackman	Jagg	Jakeman
	Jakes	Jaxon	

The surname Jackson, meaning 'son of Jack', stems from the first name Jack, but it is difficult to know whether Jack is a derivative of John or of Jacques (French for James). Certainly most of the diminutive forms, Jacklin, Jackett, Jaggard and so on, are from James (which see).

There are many early references to Jack and its diminutives. One Andreas filius Jake appears in the 1195–97 Pipe Rolls for Cornwall, while a Jakelinus is recorded in Yorkshire in the Book of Fees dated 1219. The earliest reference to the name Jackson itself appears in the 1327 Subsidy Rolls for Suffolk, where one Adam Jackessone is listed.

A JACKSON MISCELLANY

Jacksons seem to be born fighters. John 'Gentleman' Jackson (1769–1845) was a famous barefisted pugilist who held the English championship for eight years, then retired in 1803 to coach Lord Byron, amongst others. Peter Jackson (1861–1901), the first great black boxer, won both the Australian heavyweight title (1886) and the British Empire title (1892) while Henry Jackson is the real name of Henry Armstrong (b. 1912), the only man to have held three world boxing championships simultaneously: featherweight (1937), welterweight (1938) and lightweight (1938).

*

The renowned English test cricketer, Sir Stanley Jackson (1870–1947), played against Australia in the famous 1893 series, then went on to become Governor of Bengal as well as Chairman of the Conservative Party.

*

The 1901 Jacksonville, Florida fire destroyed a total of over 1700 buildings.

*

American President Andrew Jackson (1767–1845) originated the ubiquitous American slang expression 'OK'. Jackson's grammar and spelling were as rough as his frontier origins. Therefore he approved presidential papers with the notation 'OK', his way of abbreviating 'Oll Korrect'.

*

The 'Major Mite', whose real name was William E. Jackson (1864–1900), was one of the world's shortest dwarfs. He was only 27 in (70 cm) tall. On the other hand, another Jackson, Baby Flo (Mrs Flora Mae Jackson), weighed over 60 stone just before her death in 1965.

*

There are no Jackson-related towns or major geographic features in the United Kingdom. Canada's Newfoundland has a town called Jackson's Arm, New Zealand has a Jackson Head (as well as a town called Jacksons) and South Africa has a Jackson's Drift. Australia has a town called simply Jackson, as do no fewer than 16 states of America where 30 towns and cities are name related, including the well-known Jacksonville, Florida (one of 9 Jacksonvilles). Mountains in Western Australia and the United States are called Jackson, as are bays in Canada and New Zealand.

*

With about 165,000 namesakes Jackson is the 24th most popular surname in England and Wales. (The name is not common enough throughout Scotland to be counted separately.) Jackson is notably popular in and around Leeds where an estimated one in about 215 families bears the name. In descending numerical order Sheffield, Teesside and Bradford are other Jackson strongholds. Around the world Jacksons are most common in Auckland (one in 592 families), Wellington (one in 607) and Sydney (one in 701). The

United States has more Jacksons than the entire combined populations of Bristol and Southampton – an estimated total of just over 661,000 makes this their 17th most popular surname.

JAMES

RELATED NAMES

Other surnames which are related as to root, derivation or usage include:

Gemmes, Jacob, Jacobs, Jacobson, Jacoby, Jacques, Jago, Jagoe, Jakes, Jameson, Jamie, Jamieson, Jamison, Jayme, Jeames, Jem, Jemme

The surname James derived directly from the first name. This in its turn is a form of the original Hebrew name Jacob, and first became popular through the two Apostles. The Hebrew Jacob comes from the word 'aqob' which means 'supplanter' or 'usurper' (all too appropriate in the case of Jacob, the son of Isaac – one of the earliest Jacobs – who deprived his brother Esau of his birthright).

The original Jacob became Latinised to Jacobus, and from this we get the French first name Jacques, as well as the identical Welsh and Spanish form Iago. The Latinised form later became Jacomus, and it is from this root that we get our name James. It is also the source of the Spanish form Jayme (Jaime), the Italian Giacomo, and the Irish version Seamus (pronounced Shaymus).

The name, in all its varied forms, began to gain popularity all over Europe during the twelfth and thirteenth centuries. It has been suggested that the name came to prominence around this time as a result of its having been brought back by the Crusaders, and this may have been a contributory factor.

The surname James has several variations, the most widespread being Jameson, Jamison, and Jamieson (which almost certainly derives from the Scottish abbreviation 'Jamie').

References to the name James start occurring in the English records around the turn of the twelfth century. One of the earliest of these is a certain Jam de Sancto Hylario who appears in the Early Charters for Northamptonshire for 1173–6.

The surname James is popular all over England (despite the closely related Jamisons being found almost exclusively in the Scottish lowland region). The greatest concentrations of James are now found in the West Country.

A JAMES MISCELLANY

The 'King James Version' is another name given to the Authorised Version of the Bible which was ordered by King James I. The resonant style of this classic translation remains one of the finest examples of our language.

*

Jakes was a popular Elizabethan slang word for a lavatory – which accounts for the word's frequent sly appearances in Shakespeare's comedies. The word survives in our language today as 'the Jacks', a slang expression with the same meaning.

*

'BBC English' was created by the British phonetician, Arthur Lloyd James (1884–1943), who was the arbiter on all matters of pronunciation during the Corporation's formative years.

*

Jesse James (1847–82) and his brother Frank were legendary Wild West desperadoes and bank robbers. Together they gunned down at least ten men.

*

Jameson's Raid (29 December 1895) was Doctor Leander Starr Jameson's ill-fated attempt to overthrow the Transvaal Republic by fomenting an uprising in Johannesburg. Mounted with Cecil Rhodes' backing, Jameson and his fellow soldiers of fortune were surrounded and surrendered abjectly before they ever reached the city.

*

The United Kingdom has a Jameston and 3 Jamestowns. Canada and South Africa also have Jamestowns while 10 states of America have towns and cities bearing this name. In all, 18 US locations are name related. The name is geographically common around the world, including South Africa's Jameson Park.

*

With about 127,000 namesakes James is the 40th most popular surname in England and Wales. (The name is not common enough throughout Scotland to be counted separately.) James is notably popular in and around Cardiff where an estimated one in about 115 families bears the name. In descending numerical order Bristol, Birmingham and Coventry are other James strongholds. Around the world James's are most common in Sydney (one in 709 families), Melbourne (one in 769) and Wellington (one in 893). The United States has more James's than the entire population of Southampton – an estimated total of just over 227,000 makes this their 89th most popular surname.

JOHNSON

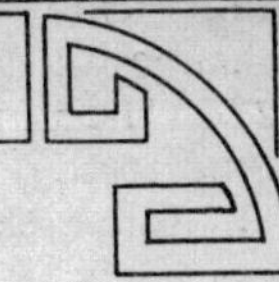

RELATED NAMES

Other surnames which are related as to root, derivation or usage include:

Fitzjohn	Jan	Jehan	John
Hancock	Janet	Jenkin	Johncock
Hanken	Janks	Jenkins	Johncook
Hankin	Jann	Jenkinson	Johnes
Hann	Janson	Jenks	Johns
Henkin	Jaynes	Jennings	Johnsen
Jack	Jeakins	Jinkin	Johnston
Jackson (which see)	Jean	Johan	Johnstone
Johnys	Joinsen	Joynson	

The surname Johnson has two main subdivisions – one with, and one without, the intrusive 't' (as in Johnstone). Both of these subdivisions have a wide variety of different spellings. The former often means 'son of John', while those variations with the 't' often refer to places – 'tons' named after John, notably in Scotland. In practice (and often in spelling) it is easy to see how the 't' got lost in pronouncing the name.

The first name John derives from the Ancient Hebrew name Jochanaan, meaning 'God is gracious'. In its Latin form the name Johannes came west with the returning Crusaders, and during the twelfth and thirteenth centuries it spread all over Europe. Doubtless it was assisted by the popularity of St John the Baptist and St John the Divine (author of the Book of Revelations).

As the name Johannes crossed national and linguistic borders, it became changed into many local variants. In Germany it became Hans, in Holland Jan, in France Jean, in Ireland Sean (pronounced Shawn), and in Scotland Jock.

Early reference to Johnsons began appearing in the English records around the thirteenth century. One John Jonessone appears in the Ancient Deeds for Surrey in 1287. Variations with the intrusive middle 't' appeared early on to denote

'John from the place ('ton' or 'tun')'. One Alan de Johannestun appears in the Assize Rolls for Staffordshire in 1227. The variations with the intrusive 't' are more common in the north of England and in Scotland.

In some rare cases the name Johnstone may be a local name deriving from places in Staffordshire and Dumfriesshire (the second syllable in this case being Old English). It is also just possible that this name is a local name for a man from Perth which used to be called St Johnstone (as its football team still is).

The name Johnson is related to the surname Evans (which also means, literally, 'the dependant of John' – see Evans) and also in this way to many widely differing names – from Jackson to Jones. Jack, like Jenkin, Hankin and Hancock, was a common pet form of John.

A JOHNSON MISCELLANY

Andrew Johnson (1808–75) was the seventeenth President of the United States. He purchased Alaska from the Russians for just $7,200,000 in 1867.

*

The three founders of the firm of Rolls-Royce were the Hon. C.S. Rolls, Mr F. Henry Royce and Mr Claude Johnson. Having at first contemplated calling the car the Rolls-Royce-Johnson, they decided that it somehow lacked zip and the name Johnson was dropped.

*

The 1889 flood in Johnstown, Pennsylvania, ranks amongst the world's all-time disasters. When the South Fork Dam broke after excessive rain, the 450-acre lake vanished in under 40 minutes as a 70-foot-high wall of water roared through the town at over 15 miles per hour. One in 10 of the citizens (well over 2,000 people) was killed and the town was virtually levelled. Johnstown was rebuilt, but in 1977 a freak storm deposited 9 inches of rain in 8 hours and the Laurel Run dam broke, releasing over 100 million gallons of water with the resultant deaths of 77 people, totally destroyed over 500 houses and caused over $200 million in damage.

*

Famed aviatrix Amy Johnson (1903–41) captured the

imagination of the nation with her record-breaking solo flight to Australia in 1930 – so much so that the song 'Wonderful Amy, How Can You Blame Me for Loving You?' was the smash hit of the year.

*

Samuel Johnson (1709–84) took a mere eight years (1747–55) to write his famous dictionary of the English language.

*

The United Kingdom has towns named Johnston, Johnstone and Johnstone Bridge, Canada has a Johnsen's Crossing and a Johnstown, New Zealand has a Johnsonville, and there are also Johnstowns in the United States (4) and Ireland (2). There is a Johnson Island off the coast of Chile, a Johnson's Point in Antigua, and a Johnson mountain range as well as a group of lakes in Australia.

*

With about 231,000 namesakes Johnson is the 10th most popular surname in England and Wales. There are over 29,000 Johnstons in Scotland where the name is 12th in popularity. In Ireland it is estimated that, with about 16,000 Johnsons, it is the 33rd most popular surname. Johnson is notably popular in and around Teesside where an estimated one in about 160 families bears the name; it is also popular in Edinburgh (one in 195). Around the world Johnsons and Johnstons are most common in Vancouver (one in 183 families), Sydney (one in 224) and Canberra (one in 228). The United States has more Johnsons and Johnstons than the entire population of Clydeside – an estimated total of just over 2,053,000 makes this their 2nd most popular surname.

JONES

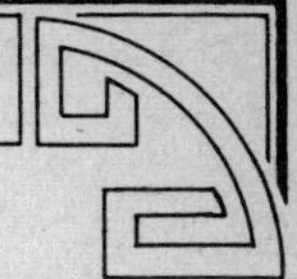

RELATED NAMES

Other surnames which are related as to root, derivation or usage include:

Fitzjones Joan Joanes John
Joynes see also Johnson

The surname Jones literally means 'dependant of John', and Jone was a common form of the Christian name in England. In Wales, John had the characteristic form Evan (see Evans), but the Welsh Authorised Bible popularised a more latinate form Ioan, which gave rise to the patronymic Jones in Wales, where it is exceptionally common.

The first name John is Hebrew in origin and means 'God is gracious' (for further details see *Johnson*).

Jones has many related variants, which range from John to Joan, Joynes to Fitzjones (son of Jones). Like Jones, most of these variants have particularly strong Welsh connections.

References to the surname Jones appear in many of the early records, but more often than not the earliest references are to its related names. Thus one Alanus filius Jene appears in the 1275 annals of Lincolnshire, and there are several Johannes in the same records. However, in 1279 the more recognisable name of Walterus filius Jone appears in the annals for Huntingdonshire, and from then on the name Jones becomes a regular feature in our records, proliferating all over the country – though still retaining its highest concentrations in South Wales.

A JONES MISCELLANY

The phrase 'Keeping up with the Joneses', which originated in a 1913 American strip cartoon, gathered strength during the decades after World War II, with the new prosperity and subsequent proliferation of snobbery.

*

The most remunerative British television contract was signed in 1968 by the singer Tom Jones, with ABC-TV of the US and ITV of London, for a reported £9 million. It stipulated that Jones was to appear in 17 one-hour shows each year between January 1969 and January 1975 – just under £90,000 an hour.

*

The Dow Jones Industrial Average Index measures the rise and fall of stocks and shares on the New York and American stock exchanges. It was instituted in 1896 by Charles Henry Dow and Edward D. Jones, former financial journalists who together, in 1882, founded the Wall Street firm of Dow Jones and Co. The British equivalent is the Financial Times Share Index.

*

'On your Jack Jones' is Cockney rhyming slang for 'on your own'.

*

Casey Jones (1864–1900) is the legendary hero commemorated in the famous ballad of the same name for his heroism as the engineer on the 'Cannonball Express'.

*

There are no Jones-related towns or major geographic features in the United Kingdom. The only towns bearing this name are in the United States where there are 19, including 9 Jonesboros and 6 Jonesvilles. A portion of the Atlantic Ocean's floor is known as Jones Bank, and Canada has a Jones Sound.

*

With about 688,000 namesakes Jones is the 2nd most popular surname in England and Wales. There are 8,000 Jones's in Scotland where it is 95th in popularity. Jones is notably popular in and around Cardiff where an estimated one in about 25 families bears the name. In descending numerical order Liverpool, Birmingham and Coventry are other Jones strongholds. Around the world Jones's are most common in Sydney (one in 224 families), Canberra (one in 256) and Melbourne (one in 289). The United States has more Jones's than the entire population of South Yorkshire – an estimated total of just over 1,400,000 makes this their 5th most popular surname.

KELLY

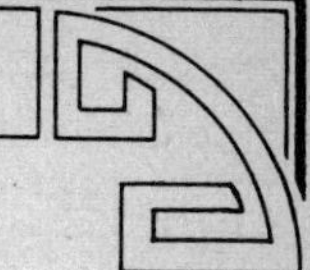

RELATED NAMES

Other surnames which are related as to root, derivation or usage include:

Keller	Kellie	Killie	McKelly
Kelley	Kellye	MacKelly	O'Kelly

Normally the surname Kelly comes from the Gaelic O'Ceallaigh. Apart from this fact the origins of the name Kelly – at least in Ireland, where it is most numerous – are obscure. One possible derivation is from the Gaelic word 'ceallach' which means 'conflict, strife or war'. If this is so, Kelly would be a nickname, the original Kelly probably achieving renown as a great fighter.

Kellys are found all over Ireland – and indeed, with emigration, all over the world. (From Boston and New York to Sydney, the local telephone directories have pages of Kellys.) The main family clan of the Kellys is native to mid-Galway and south Roscommon, but other separate family clans have their origins in Leix, Wicklow, Meath and Derry.

Kellys also come from the Isle of Man and Scotland – but almost all of these are due to early emigration. Exceptions are rare, but nonetheless these do exist. In Scotland the name Kelly is sometimes a place name, being given to natives of the town of Kelly in Angus and to those from the village of Killie in Fife. These places get their names from the Scots Gaelic or the Cornish words for 'woods'. It is also just possible that the Irish Kellys – at least in part – derive their name from a similar source in Irish Gaelic. In this case the Irish name could also be a place name, rather than the more heroic nickname. Kelly is also an old surname in Devon. In the Pipe Rolls for Devon in 1194 one Warin de Kelly is listed, named after the Devon village, and this is the first note of a Kelly in English records.

A KELLY MISCELLANY

In 1888 James Kelly, the Liverpool wife-murderer, escaped from Broadmoor, the celebrated top-security prison for mental patients in Berkshire. He did so by making a passkey from a corset spring. After his escape he lived in Paris, then in New York for many years, eluding all attempts to recapture him. Finally, he returned in 1928 to the gates of Broadmoor and asked for readmission. This was granted, and he died an inmate in 1930. No one else has ever escaped and remained free from Broadmoor for anything approaching this period.

*

Helen Adams Keller (1880–1968) became blind, deaf and dumb as a baby. By sheer persistence and with the devoted help of Anne Sullivan, she overcame these overwhelming handicaps to graduate *cum laude* from Radcliffe College, Cambridge (US). She became an inspiration to many similarly handicapped, and her autobiography, *The Story of My Life* (1902), remains widely read.

*

The sixteenth-century alchemist's assistant, Edward Kelley, claimed that he could confer with the angels by use of the magic crystals belonging to his master, John Dee. Kelley eventually persuaded his master to adopt a community of wives.

*

HMS *Kelly* was the first command of Lord Louis Mountbatten (1900–79). Later to become Viceroy of India, Earl Mountbatten earned the undying respect of his men as a result of his bravery at the time of the engagement during which HMS *Kelly* was finally sunk. He knew the name of every man on board, and refused rescue before his wounded shipmates had been assisted.

*

The first full-length film, *The Story of the Kelly Gang*, was made in Australia in 1906.

*

The United Kingdom has towns called Kelly and Kelly Bay. Other countries with name-related towns include Australia (Kelly), the US (3 Kellys), South Africa (Kelly's View) and

Ireland (Kelly's Grove). There are Kelly rivers in Alaska and Australia and Kelly lakes in Angola and Canada, as well as Kelly Hills in Australia.

*

With about 58,000 namesakes Kelly is the 2nd most popular surname in Ireland. There are over 16,000 Kellys in Scotland where it is 40th in popularity. (The name is not common enough throughout England and Wales to be counted separately.) Around the world Kellys are most common in Canberra (one in 354 families), Sydney (one in 593) and Ottawa (one in 637). The United States has more Kellys than the entire population of Hull – an estimated total of just under 275,000 makes this their 61st most popular surname.

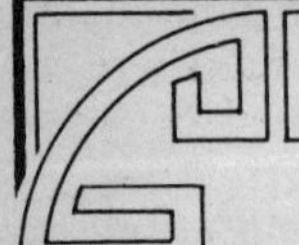

KING

RELATED NAMES

Other surnames which are related as to root, derivation or usage include:

Kingdom	Kingman	Kingshott	Kingsmill
Kinge	Kings	Kingsland	Kingsnorth
Kingett	Kingsbury	Kingsley	Kingson
Kinggett	Kingsford	Kingsman	Kingston
Kingstone	Kington	Kingwell	

The surname King has two origins. One is the Old English word Cyng, 'a king', which was used in Old English times as a personal name and may have given rise to a surname. The other, and by far the more common, is a nickname 'king' found in many villages in medieval England. Experts believe that the most common designation of the name was for men who governed the rituals of harvest-time in medieval villages. Sometimes these rites were celebrated with annual pageants and masques, where the same parts were often taken by the same individual year after year. Thus he who played the part of king often found the name attached to him.

Alternatively the nickname may have been an ironic reference to the overbearing, swaggering manner of someone in the village. Or it may have been used as an occupational name for someone in the King's service – i.e. a servant of the King, a King's messenger, or sometimes simply a tax collector.

In extremely rare cases, it is thought that the name King was given to an illegitimate offspring of royal descent. However, many authorities doubt whether this ever happened.

The surname King has many related names. Most of them are place names – given to someone who came from a particular place. The best known of these are Kingsbury (places in Middlesex and Somerset), Kingsford (Hampshire and Suffolk), and Kingston (the official name of Hull, and the town in Surrey).

Variants on the name King appear in many of the early

records, but perhaps the earliest reference to the name as we know it is in the Pipe Rolls for Cambridgeshire. There in 1177 one Geoffrey King is mentioned.

A KING MISCELLANY

Martin Luther King (1929–68) was the black American civil rights leader whose example did more to advance his people's rights than any other of his generation. In 1964 he was awarded the Nobel Peace Prize, but just four years later was killed by an assassin's bullet.

*

British botanist Francis Ward Kingdon (1885–1958) discovered and began cultivation of the Himalayan blue poppy. In half a century of pioneering expeditions he made 25 journeys to the eastern Himalayas.

*

Unconventional Louisiana governor Huey Long was nicknamed 'The Kingfish' by his poverty-stricken adulatory followers, to signify his supremacy in their affections.

*

American politician John Alsop King persuaded the 1855 state convention of the Whig Party to adopt 'Republican' as the party's name. It has remained that ever since.

*

William Mackenzie King (1874–1950) was Canada's Prime Minister a remarkable three times during his 30 years as head of the Liberal Party.

*

President Charles King of Liberia was elected into office in 1928 by a massive 600,000 majority. It was an amazing feat in a country whose electorate was then just 15,000.

*

King takes pride of place when it comes to name-related towns, cities and geographic features. In all, 106 towns and cities in the United Kingdom are King-related. These range from Kingarth to Kingswelton and include 9 Kingstons and 7 Kingswoods. The US has 45 such towns and cities, Canada has 4, Australia 10, New Zealand 2, and South Africa 5. Kingston is Jamaica's capital. Numerous geographic features bear the generic name or are named for specific kings (King

George's Reservoir, King Edward River, King Lear Mountain, King Leopold range, etc.)

*

With about 136,000 namesakes King is the 34th most popular surname in England and Wales. There are over 7,000 Kings in Scotland where it is 98th in popularity. In Ireland it is estimated that with about 9,000, King is the 86th most popular surname. King is notably popular in and around Bristol where an estimated one in about 368 families bears the name. In descending numerical order Leicester, London and Coventry are other King strongholds. Around the world Kings are most common in Sydney (one in 499 families), Auckland (one in 520) and Wellington (one in 524). The United States has more Kings than the entire population of Bristol – an estimated total of just over 456,000 makes this their 28th most popular surname.

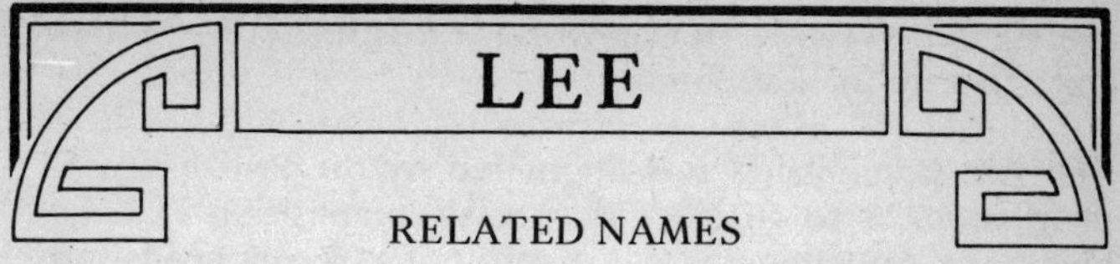

LEE

RELATED NAMES

Other surnames which are related as to root, derivation or usage include:

Atlee	Lea	Lees	Ley
Lay	Leabrook	Legh	Leys
Laye	Leagh	Leigh	Lye

The surname Lee is a variant of Lea. This is a place name coming from the Old English word 'leah', which means 'wood, glade, clearing, field or pasture'. The related surnames Legh and Leigh are usually from the Middle English form of the word, 'legh' – though they do occasionally derive from the older source. However, contrary to appearances, these latter Leighs (and Leghs) are not closer derivations of the Old English source than the Lees and Leas. 'Lea' is the dative of the Old English 'Leah', and was used after prepositions such as 'at' or 'in'. It was common practice to refer to someone who lived by a particular place as living 'at' it – as, for example, in John at Lee. Thus we get the name Atlee.

Other variations on the name come from the Old English 'laege' meaning 'fallow', and 'laes' meaning 'meadow'. These include Ley, Leys, Laye, Lye, Lees, and such obvious rural compounds as Leabrook.

Early references to Lee abound in the records from the twelfth century onwards, and are found all over England. One of the earliest is to an Ailric de la Leie, who appears in the early Charters for Norfolk covering the years 1148–66.

A LEE MISCELLANY

Gypsy Rose Lee (1904–70) was the greatest strip-tease artist of them all, bringing wit, style and grace to this profession unmatched since Salome. After retiring she wrote the best-selling autobiography *Gypsy*, and then wrote two further best-sellers *The G-String Murders* (1941) and *Mother finds a Body* (1942). During World War II she returned to the stage to strip for war-bonds.

*

The Lee Commission was appointed by the British Government in 1923 to consider the racial composition of India's higher government services. As a result of its recommendations, when India became independent in 1947 over half of the 1,000 members of these services were Indians with long experience.

*

Lee's Professor is the holder of one of three chairs at Oxford.

*

England's Prime Ministers, past and present, owe a debt of gratitude to Arthur Hamilton Lee – he left them his estate, Chequers, for use as a country house.

*

Poet and novelist Laurie Lee based books like *Cider with Rosie* and *As I Walked Out One Midsummer Morning* on his deep love and understanding of rural Gloucestershire, where he grew up.

*

Manfred B. Lee is better known by his pseudonym, Ellery Queen. Together with Frederic Dannay, he wrote murder mysteries which often featured a break just before the end, inviting the reader to see if he could solve the crime before the fictional detective announced the solution.

*

Lees seem to have a predilection for achieving fame on the stage. Amongst the best known of these are Christopher Lee, maestro of the Hammer horror films, Bruce Lee the great Kung Fu hero, and Vivien Leigh, one-time wife of Laurence Olivier, who played Scarlett O'Hara in *Gone With The Wind*.

*

Robert E. Lee was the only general in history to have been offered the command of both armies in a war. He turned down the offer of the Union command and went on to become the legendary leader of the Southern Army during the American Civil War.

His family produced several other outstanding military commanders. Robert's father, Henry 'Light-Horse' Lee, was a close aide to George Washington, and Henry's eldest son, also called Henry, distinguished himself in the War of 1812.

*

English clergyman William Lee (1550–1610) invented the first knitting machine. The woman he was courting showed far more interest in knitting than in his attentions, and this was his solution.

*

A total of 25 towns and cities in the United Kingdom are related to this name including 5 towns called Lee, 2 Leeds, and 2 named Lees. While Canada is Lee-less the United States has 26 name-related towns and cities. Denmark also has a town called Lee. The name is geographically common.

*

With about 119,000 namesakes Lee is the 42nd most popular surname in England and Wales. (The name is not common enough throughout Scotland to be counted separately.) Lee is notably popular in and around Sheffield where an estimated one in about 415 families bears the name. In descending numerical order Bradford, Leeds and Nottingham are other Lee strongholds. Around the world Lees are most common in Vancouver (one in 308 families), Toronto (one in 419) and Sydney (one in 547). The United States has more Lees than the entire population of Bristol – an estimated total of just under 429,000 makes this their 35th most popular surname.

LEWIS

RELATED NAMES

Other surnames which are related as to root, derivation or usage include:

Leuis	Lewison	Lewys	Louis
Lewisohn	Lewse	Llewelyn	Lowis

The surname Lewis began life as a first name. It means 'renowned or famous in battle', and its original form was first found in Germany where it is now found in the form Ludwig. When the name crossed to France as Lowis or Louis, it soon became popular. This popularity increased through the centuries, as we can see from the fact that France had no fewer than eighteen kings called Louis, one of whom even became a saint. As the name Louis spread beyond the borders of France it changed once more. In Italy it became Luigi, and by the time it came to England with the Norman invasion it had become Lewis.

In this form the name gradually spread across the entire country, although being originally a foreign name it never achieved the same popularity as it achieved in France. Why, then, are there now so many Lewis's? The answer to this question lies in their distribution.

Lewis's have existed for many centuries throughout all the English counties, and in Wales they are extremely plentiful. The theory which best accounts for the proliferation of Welsh Lewis's is that the Welsh name Lewis is in fact an attempted anglicisation of the Welsh name Llewelyn. (In times of persecution, when Wales was only a princedom under repression, many Welshmen found it expedient to change their name to a more English form.) This theory may sound rather far-fetched, but it would appear to be confirmed by the earliest reference we have to the name Lewis. In the 1413 records the Alderman of Brecon is given as 'Llewelyn ap-Madoc, alias Lewis Rede'. By then Lewis was certainly a widespread and popular name and over 100 years later it crops up in Shakespeare, a distinction shared by very few of the more popular British names. Among these few are two other predominantly Welsh names: Thomas and Griffith.

There are several names which derive directly or indirectly from Lewis. The best known of these are Leuis, Lowis, Lewse – all being simply variations in spelling dating from the times before spelling was formalised. (Lewison, from 'son of Lewis', is also popular.) However, the similar-looking name of Lewes is not a variation of Lewis. It is a local name, deriving from the town in Sussex, and means 'hills or mounds', referring to the Downs among which the town lies.

Another origin of the name Lewis results from the eastern European pogroms of the last century. During this time many Jews crossed over to England and on arrival decided to anglicise their names. A number of refugees with the name Levinsky changed it to Lewin, Levin or Lewis.

Owing to its popularity in Britain and France – two of Europe's major colonising nations – the name Lewis (or Louis) has spread around the globe. Over the centuries it has been particularly popular in the United States. Here we find it in St Louis, in Louisville, and even in the State of Louisiana (which, under French colonial rule – before the famous Louisiana Purchase in 1803 – stretched from the coast of the Gulf of Mexico up into the Mid-West, to within a few hundred miles of the Great Lakes).

In America, because of this early pervasive French influence, the French spelling of Louis is still more popular than the Anglo-Welsh Lewis (e.g. Louis Armstrong), so much so that its popularity as a first name in this French form has even spread back across the Atlantic, but this time to England.

A LEWIS MISCELLANY

The American explorer Meriwether Lewis (1774–1809) led the great overland journey to the Pacific coast, thus opening up the north-west to a flood of settlers. Despite encounters with grizzly bears, Indians, rattlesnakes and near-starvation Lewis's only brush with death came when a hunting companion mistook him for an elk and shot him in the leg.

As a reward for his explorations he was appointed the first governor of Louisiana but died soon after in mysterious circumstances.

*

The first machine-gun was invented by the American Isaac Newton Lewis (1858–1931). The American military brass proved uninterested in his new invention so he took it to Europe in 1913 where the Lewis Gun played a vital part in the last stages of World War I. Over 100,000 were manufactured for the Allied armies by the Birmingham Small Arms Company.

*

Many Lewis's have achieved fame as writers. The first American to win the Nobel Prize was Sinclair Lewis, whose best-seller *Main Street* swept him to fame. C. Day Lewis (1904–72) was one of the 'Thirties Poets' of Auden's generation. He later became Poet Laureate. The controversial writer-artist Percy Wyndham Lewis founded the English modernist movement called Vorticism, which created a furore prior to World War I. The prolific scholar-writer C.S. Lewis is best remembered for his *Screwtape Letters*.

*

Lewis's have produced several jazz greats. George Lewis was a veteran of the Old New Orleans style and John Lewis, the composer-pianist, recorded with Charlie Parker and Dizzy Gillespie.

*

The United Kingdom has a Lewisham (along with South Africa), a Lewis, a Lewiston and a Butt of Lewis. A total of 22 United States towns and cities are Lewis-related. Both Australia and the US have Lewis Ranges and the name is geographically common.

*

With about 179,000 namesakes Lewis is the 19th most popular surname in England and Wales. (The name is not common enough throughout Scotland to be counted separately.) Lewis is notably popular in and around Cardiff where an estimated one in about 70 families bears the name. In descending numerical order Bristol, Birmingham and Coventry are other Lewis strongholds. Around the world

Lewis's are most common in Sydney (one in 701 families), Melbourne (one in 761) and Capetown (one in 915). The United States has more Lewis's than the entire population of Sunderland – an estimated total of just under 520,000 makes this their 20th most popular surname.

MacCARTHY

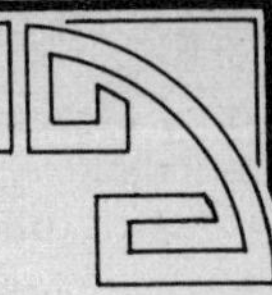

RELATED NAMES

Other surnames which are related as to root, derivation or usage include:

Craddock Cradduck Cradick MacCartie
McCarthy

The Irish surname MacCarthy comes from the Gaelic MacCarthaigh. This surname originates from the first name Carthach, which means 'loving'. As well as being the thirteenth most popular name in Ireland, it is also the most popular 'Mac' name. The MacCarthys have played an heroic part in Irish history throughout the ages, and are one of the leading family clans of Munster.

This simple explanation of the origin of MacCarthy omits a number of complicating but interesting variations en route. MacCarthy also means 'son of Craddock' – a form of the name Carthach (or Carthaigh) – and an earlier form of Craddock was Caratacus. This renowned Ancient British name is perhaps more recognisable as the Welsh Caradoc. Caratacus (or Caradoc) was a famous British chieftain of the Catuvellauni, who resisted so nobly against the Romans between 37–43 AD. Finally, around 50 AD, he was captured and together with his family he was shipped to Rome in chains. Here, amongst other indignities which befell him, Caratacus had his name Latinised to Caractacus (and as such he appears in the popular song).

The name which derives most directly from Caradoc is the Welsh surname Craddock. In its early form this name appears in the 1177 Pipe Rolls for Hereford, where one Caradoc is listed.

It was over a century later that MacCarthy (or 'son of Craddock') began to appear. The earliest mention of this name is of one Douenald Roth' Mackarthi in the Patent Rolls for 1285.

A MacCARTHY MISCELLANY

McCarthys have played a large part in post-war American politics. Infamous US Senator Joseph McCarthy (1908–57) captured national headlines in the early 1950s with his sensational claim that Communists had infiltrated the highest levels of government, especially the State Department. Although he never actually produced the name of one 'card-carrying Communist', the witch-hunt whipped up a national hysteria that destroyed many careers. McCarthy's power finally declined after a lengthy 1954 televised hearing in which top civilians and military brass were cross-examined in front of an audience of millions. McCarthy, always a heavy drinker, finally died a broken alcoholic.

Another US Senator, Eugene McCarthy (b. 1916), made a bid for the 1968 presidential nomination against the incumbent, Lyndon B. Johnson. Though unsuccessful, he mobilised political idealism and anti-Vietnam War sentiments. As such he was influential in Johnson's decision not to seek re-relection.

*

A descendant of Blarney Castle's fifteenth-century builder, Cormac MacCarthy gave the English language a new term for slippery eloquence – 'blarney' – when he put off Queen Elizabeth I's demands for his allegiance with 'fair words and soft speech'.

*

Governing comes naturally to the MacCarthys. Sir Charles MacCarthy was Governor of the Gold Coast until he was killed in the Ashanti in 1824. MacCarthy's Island, originally a site for freed slaves, off the West African coast is named for him. In the eighteenth century a MacCarthy was Governor of Madras, and in the nineteenth century Sir Charles Justin MacCarthy was Governor of Ceylon.

*

A MacCarthy – Colonel Daniel E. – was the first American soldier to set foot in France in 1917.

*

Geographic and urban namesakes are all but non-existent. There is one town called McCarthy in Alaska.

*

In Ireland with about 23,000 namesakes McCarthy is the 13th most popular surname. (In England, Scotland and Wales McCarthy is not common enough to be counted separately.) Around the world McCarthys and MacCarthys are most common in Canberra (one in 1,278 families), Sydney (one in 1,338) and Auckland (one in 1,391). In the United States there are an estimated 161,000 McCarthys and MacCarthys – in combination, making this the country's 142nd most popular surname.

MacDONALD

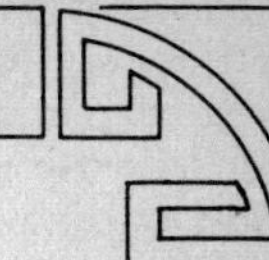

RELATED NAMES

Other surnames which are related as to root, derivation or usage include:

Donald Donaldson MacConnell MacDonell MacDonnell McDonald

The surname MacDonald means 'descendant of Donald' and comes from the Scots Gaelic Mac Dhomhnuill. The origin of the first name Dhomhnuill was a nickname meaning no less than 'world ruler'. Not being a backward modest people, the Scots adopted this name in large numbers, and it soon became one of the most popular first names in the land, being held by several kings and one saint (in the ninth century). The abbreviation Don also became widespread, though the formal Donal is more an Irish usage.

According to George Black, the greatest expert on Scottish names, strictly speaking there is no such name as MacDonald, (because the Gaelic Mac Dhomhnuill really means 'son of a *particular* Donald'). This holds true for all the 'Mac' names.

The MacDonalds are one of the major Scottish clans, whose chieftains are descended directly from Donald, son of Reginald (Old Norse Ragnaldr), second son of the great Somerled (Old Norse Sumarlithr), Lord of the Isles, so the line is ultimately Scandinavian. The Scots Gaelic name for the clan is Clann Domhnuill. The clan can claim to be the most numerous and widespread of all the Scottish clans. However, not all clan members are of pure descent – through the centuries the Clan MacDonald absorbed several minor family clans and 'broken' men (who had left or 'broken from' their own clans).

A popular verbal variant of the original MacDonald is the name MacConnell, which is found particularly in Ulster. Another popular variant name is MacDonell. Yet these are the tip of the iceberg compared with the many variations in the ancient records which tried to transliterate from the original Gaelic. These range from Maconhale (1588) through McConnil (1564) to M'Donnyle (1326). Fortunately, most of these variants have now become absorbed into the more standard forms. The earliest reference to the name in any form in the records is in the Dublin lists for 1257, where one Robert Dovenald appears.

A MacDONALD MISCELLANY

McDonald's hamburger chain, the largest restaurant group in the world with nearly 6,000 restaurants in 25 countries, was founded by brothers Maurice and Richard McDonald whose parents emigrated to the United States from County Mayo. Since the first outlet opened in 1948 the company has sold over 22 billion hamburgers. Sales in one year alone totalled over £2,287 million.

*

Alistair MacDonnell, called 'Pickle the Spy', was a Scottish chieftain of dubious integrity employed by Highland leaders on a secret mission to Charles Stuart, Pretender to the English throne. When captured by the English, he promptly switched his allegiance and agreed to spy on the Prince.

*

MacDonalds have had a way of getting to the top in politics. Ramsay MacDonald, an illegitimate child who grew up in poverty and left school at the age of 12, overcame these handicaps to become Britain's first Labour Prime Minister. Two John MacDonalds have been Prime Ministers of Canada: Sir John A. MacDonald, as Canada's first Prime Minister, is known as 'the father of Confederation', while Prime Minister John Sandfield Macdonald, unlike Sir John, violently opposed federation.

*

Scottish-born Sir James Ronald Leslie Macdonald, soldier and explorer, first made a geographical exploration of British East Africa (now Kenya and Uganda), and later mapped the Lake Victoria area.

*

MacDonalds have been notable for getting into tight spots, then extricating themselves with great skill. After his crushing defeat at Culloden, Flora MacDonald (1722–90) helped

Bonnie Prince Charlie escape from the Hebrides dressed in her maid's clothes. The British briefly imprisoned, then pardoned, her.

Jacques-Alexandre MacDonald (1765–1840) had a brilliant career as one of Napoleon's top generals (his winter crossing of the Alps was favourably compared to Napoleon's own crossing of the St Bernard Pass). Arrested for anti-Bonapartist plots, he was regarded as so indispensable that he was pardoned and recalled to duty when France was threatened by Austria. He went on to be a Marshal of Empire and member of the Legion of Honour.

*

Sir Hector MacDonald (1853–1903) distinguished himself in the Afghan War, the Boer War and the Sudan where, as a major-general in command of Egyptian troops, he became a national hero and was voted Parliament's thanks.

*

When foreign legations in Peking were besieged by thousands of marauding Chinese during the Boxer Rebellion of 1900, British diplomat Sir Claude Maxwell Macdonald was in command.

*

The sixteenth-century Irish chieftain of Scottish descent, Sorley Boy MacDonnell, was tricked by the English into battling it out with his rival Shane O'Neill over disputed lands in Ulster. When O'Neill retaliated vigorously, MacDonnell was defeated. Twenty-two years later Sorley Boy was confirmed in his possessions by Elizabeth I and became Constable of Dunluce Castle.

*

There are no MacDonald towns or major geographic features in the United Kingdom. Around the world there are 2 towns named McDonald in the US and a MacDonald Downs in Australia. Both countries also have McDonald lakes while Australia and Canada have MacDonald Ranges. There is a MacDonald Island in the Indian Ocean and a MacDonald Rock in the Pacific.

*

With about 30,000 namesakes MacDonald and McDonald form Scotland's 2nd most popular surname – thus about one out of every 103 Scots is so named. (The name is not common enough throughout England and Wales to be counted separately.) MacDonald and McDonald are notably popular in and around Glasgow where an estimated one in about 160 families bears the name, and in Edinburgh where the figure is about one in 155. Around the world the surname is most common in Vancouver (one in 229 families), Ottawa (one in 267) Canberra (one in 324) and Toronto (one in 350). The United States has 64,000 MacDonalds and 193,000 McDonalds – the estimated combined total of 257,000 is larger than the population of two Carlisles and makes this their 68th most popular surname.

McKAY

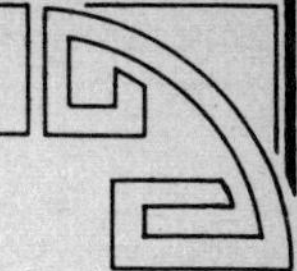

RELATED NAMES

Other surnames which are related as to root, derivation or usage include:

Mackay Mackaye Mackey Mackie
Mackieson McKee McKie

The surname McKay is of Scots origin, coming from the Scots Gaelic MacAoidh which means 'son of Aodh'. The original meaning of the first name Aodh remains uncertain, but the most probable translation is 'fire'. This would thus have been a nickname, referring probably to the temperament (or possibly the complexion or hair-colour) of the holder. Another possible translation of Aodh is 'inspiration'. This original first name is another possible origin for some instances of the popular first names of Hugh and Hugo.

The McKays originally came from the far north of Scotland, and from Inverness-shire. The origin of the main northern McKays is obscure, but they may well have come from the legendary Clann Morgan. The Inverness-shire McKays usually write their name in Gaelic as MacAi. This further complicates the origin of the name, for MacAi in Scots Gaelic is a form of MacDhai, which translated as 'Davidson' (the Scots Gaelic Dhai being similar to the popular Welsh first name 'Dai').

As is usual with names that have been translated from the Gaelic through the ages, there have been countless variations on this name in the records. These range from Mackhe (1538) to Macky (1513) and M'Akie (1559). This variation gave rise to the ancient Stirlingshire name of Mackie, and thus Mackieson. This popular form means 'son of the son of –'. The more common Macpherson is not the same – this comes from the Gaelic Mac an Phearsain, meaning 'son of the parson'.

The earliest mention of any version of McKay comes in the 1098 Manx records. Here one Cucail Mac Aedha is mentioned. However, it is not until 1326 that we find the more recognisable name Gilchrist M'Ay, who is listed by George Black, the eminent expert on Scottish names.

A McKAY MISCELLANY

The American colloquialism 'the real McCoy' (meaning 'genuine', 'best of its kind') originated through a mix-up over a brand of whisky called McKays exported to the US in the 1880s. The company slogan was confused with the name of an American boxer named McCoy.

*

Scotsman James Mackay explored the Missouri River and pushed on to the Pacific coast, drawing up the map later used by the famous Lewis and Clark expedition.

*

The enormous multi-national company International Telephone and Telegraph (IT&T) was founded by Clarence Hungerford MacKay (1874–1938) who supervised the completion of the first trans-Pacific cable between the United States and the Far East (1907).

*

The largest clipper ship ever built, the *Great Republic*, 4,555 tons, was produced by master Boston shipbuilder Donald McKay (1810–80). Not only did he make them big; he made them fast. His boatyard's ship *Lightning* had a top speed of 21 knots and established a long-standing record of 436 nautical miles in 24 hours.

*

The only two towns named McKay are in Australia and the United States. Australia has a MacKay Lake, Canada has 2 (one spelled MacKay) as well as a McKay river. Australia has a MacKay mountain and a McKay mountain range.

*

With about 25,000 namesakes MacKay and McKay form Scotland's 18th most popular surname. Thus about one out of every 208 Scots is named MacKay or McKay. (The name is not common enough throughout England and Wales to be counted separately.) MacKay and McKay are notably popular in and around both Edinburgh and Glasgow; in each an estimated one in about 240 families bears the name. Around the world this surname is most common in Wellington (one in 562 families), Canberra (one in 622), Vancouver (one in 694) and Auckland (one in 732). The United States has 11,000 MacKays and 41,000 McKays – in combination making this their 527th most popular surname.

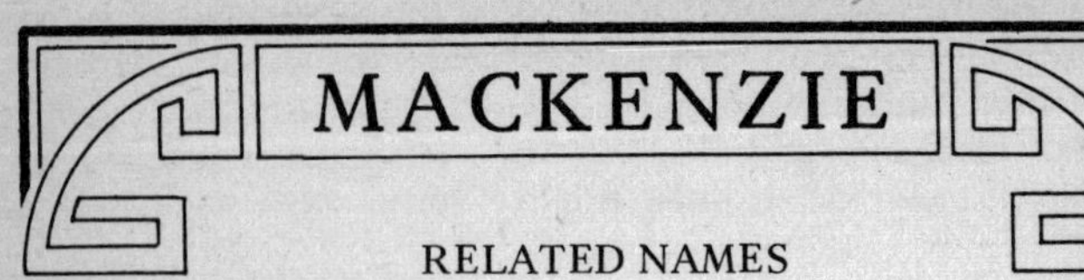

MACKENZIE

RELATED NAMES

Other surnames which are related as to root, derivation or usage include:

Kenny Kinney MacCoinneach MacCoinnig
McKenzie MacKinnie

The surname Mackenzie is of Scots origin and comes from the Scots Gaelic MacCoinnich, which means 'son of Coinneach'. This obsolete first name derives indirectly from the Gaelic word 'cann' meaning 'fair, bright or comely'. Thus, this first name originated as a nickname, describing the appearance or personality of the original holder. (The equivalent Irish Gaelic roots of this word may in some rare cases have given rise to the Irish name Kenny – though this is certainly not the main derivation.)

Mention of the name Mackenzie goes back as far as 1264, when one Makbeth Makkyneth attended the pleas held at Dull in Angus during 1264. This name may seem a long way from the Mackenzie we know, but being originally a Gaelic name, Mackenzie (or MacCoinnich) was translated into English when it was written down in the records. Because Gaelic and English are by no means parallel in pronunciation, this led to a large number of different spellings in the records. These range from M'Hunzie (1684) to M'Kenzoch (1586) and Makkunze (1513). Most of these variants have now died out, so that the name is almost invariably spelt Mackenzie – an unusual uniformity in a Gaelic-derived Scottish name.

A MACKENZIE MISCELLANY

Sir Edward Montague Compton Mackenzie (1883–1972), with over 100 novels and plays to his credit, is well known as one of Scotland's (and indeed Britain's) most prolific writers, with an output that topped one work per annum. What is less well known is that he was one of the founders of the Scottish Nationalist Party.

*

British missionary John Mackenzie (1835–99) was a dedicated champion of the rights of native Africans in nineteenth-century South Africa, and was instrumental in the British Government's move to set up Bechuanaland as a protectorate to combat Boer racialism.

*

The polygraph machine, popularly known as the 'lie detector', was the brainchild of British physician Sir James Mackenzie. When used in police work, the assumption is that a guilty suspect's respiration, blood pressure and pulse rate will increase due to nervousness when he lies.

*

Mackenzies have made a name for themselves in distant lands. Sir Alexander Mackenzie (1755–1820) traced the course of the 1,100-mile Canadian river which now bears his name to its delta the Arctic Ocean, the first known trans-continental crossing of North America above Mexico. Bishop Charles Frederick Mackenzie (1825–62) headed the Church's mission in the Zambezi River region of Central Africa and scandalised settlers by insisting that black converts had equal rights in all church affairs.

*

Canada's first Liberal Prime Minister was Alexander Mackenzie. After emigrating from Perth he swiftly rose to his new homeland's highest political office, holding the post from 1873–78. He refused a knighthood three times.

*

There are no towns, cities or major geographic features related to this name in the United Kingdom. Canada has 2 towns named Mackenzie, 2 McKenzie lakes, Mackenzie mountains and the famed Mackenzie river. The United States has 3 towns named McKenzie and a McKenzie river. New Zealand has the Mackenzie Plains while Australia has a river called Mackenzie.

*

With about 26,000 namesakes Mackenzie and McKenzie form Scotland's 15th most popular surname. Thus one out of every 200 Scots is so named. (The name is not common enough throughout England and Wales to be counted separately.) This surname is notably popular in and around

Edinburgh, where an estimated one in about 223 families bears the name, and in Glasgow where the figure is about one in 228. Around the world this surname is most common in Vancouver (one in 563 families), Wellington (one in 673), Auckland (one in 677) and Melbourne (one in 767). The United States has 11,000 Mackenzies and 41,000 McKenzies – in combination making this their 575th most popular surname.

MacLEAN

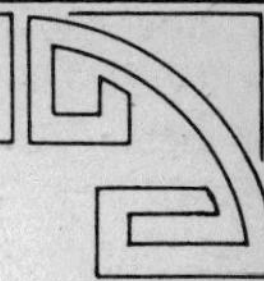

RELATED NAMES

Other surnames which are related as to root, derivation or usage include:

MacIlwaine MacLane Maclean McLaine
McLane McLean

The surname MacLean is of Scottish origin and means 'son of the devotee of (Saint) John'. The intrusive '-L' in the middle of the name is all that remains of the Scots Gaelic word 'gillie', which means 'servant, lad or follower'. This we see more clearly in the Scots Gaelic version of McLean, which is Mac Gille Eoin. Eoin is the main Gaelic version of John, and is now more usually found as Iain, a highly popular Scots first name. The original first name John comes from the Hebrew Jochanaan, which means 'God is gracious'. (For further details of history and origin of the first name John, see entry for Johnson.

The origins of the Clan McLean are clouded in spurious legends. However, it seems almost certain that the clan had two separate origins. The collective clan is known today in Gaelic as Clann 'ic 'ill Eathain.

The earliest mention of this name comes at the end of the thirteenth century, when one Gilmore Maclyn is listed as having paid homage to the King in 1296. As is usual in names translated from the Gaelic, there is a large variety of different spellings to be found in the records. These range from MacGillane (1526) to M'Gillean (1436) and M'Illclyane (sixteenth century). Most of these variations have now died out or have reverted to the standard McLean or MacLean. However, the version McLane is well known in America.

By a curious oddity, the name MacLean is also found frequently in Prussia. These MacLeans refer to themselves as the 'MacLeans of Coll' and are almost certainly of mercenary origin, though a persistent local legend has it that these MacLeans helped John MacLean, son of the laird of Dowant, to build the Swedish city of Gothenberg in the mid-seventeenth century. (In so doing, the canny Scot also accumulated a fortune, and was enrolled by Queen Christina of Sweden in 1649.)

A MacLEAN MISCELLANY

The last surviving participant in the Charge of the Light Brigade was Sir Fitzroy Donald Maclean (1835–1931). He also achieved the distinction of being the longest-lived baronet on record.

*

Britain's two most celebrated post-war spies were Guy Burgess (1911–63) and Donald Maclean (b.1913). After being tipped off by master spy Kim Philby that their cover had been blown, the pair fled to Russia, where Maclean still lives.

*

One of the most consistent best-selling authors of all time is the Scottish-born adventure writer Alistair MacLean (b.1922). Between 1955 and 1978 he averaged a book a year. No fewer than 17 of them sold over a million copies. Twelve were made into action-packed films, including *The Guns of Navarone* (1961) and *Where Eagles Dare* (1969).

*

It is a little-known fact that the American Civil War both began and ended in the same room: the front parlour of Major Wilmer McLean's house in Virginia. After the peace treaty was signed, souvenir-hunters stripped the house of all its furniture. A speculator later bought the house and dismantled it brick by brick, with the idea of re-erecting it in Washington as a tourist attraction. Unfortunately, he went bankrupt in the process, and the dismantled house has never been reassembled.

*

There are no towns, cities or major geographic features related to this name in the United Kingdom. Canada has one town named McClean, the United States has 4 (including McLean, Virginia, home of the CIA) and a McLeansboro. Australia has a MacLean and South Africa a MacLeantown. The only major geographic feature is Canada's McLean Lake.

*

With about 23,000 namesakes MacLean and McLean form Scotland's 19th most popular surname. Thus about one out of every 225 Scots is so named. (The name is not common enough throughout England and Wales to be counted separately.) This surname is notably popular in and around Glasgow where an estimated one in about 190 families bears the name, and in Edinburgh where the figure is about one in 335. Around the world MacLeans and McLeans are most common in Vancouver (one in 672 families), Ottawa (one in 836), Toronto (one in 917) and Wellington (one in 949). The United States has 43,000 McLeans which makes this variation of the name the 702nd most popular surname. They do not record MacLeans since there are fewer than 10,000 in the population.

MARTIN

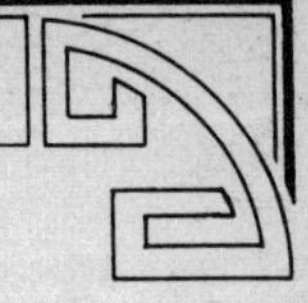

RELATED NAMES

Other surnames which are related as to root, derivation or usage include:

Kilmartin	Marten	Martenson	Martinsmith
Martell	Martens	Martins	Martinson
Marton	Martyn	Martyns	

The surname Martin derives from the popular first name. The first name Martin has ancient origins which start at the same source as the first name Mark. Both these first names derive from the Latin name Martius, which means 'of Mars'. Mars was a pagan god of war, and thus Martius was a common name for a warrior. Strictly speaking, Martin is a diminutive of Martius.

Martin owes its popularity as a Christian name to the fourth-century Saint Martin, who was originally a soldier but finally ended up as Bishop of Tours in France. His best-known act was tearing his cloak in two and giving one half to a beggar.

Occasionally, the surname Martin derives from a place name. There are in fact villages called Martin or Marten in six English counties; and from this source the surname would mean 'a person from Martin (or Marten)'. The place name means 'a place near a mere or lake'.

The most widespread variations on Martin are Marten, Martyn and Martell. The last of these is a double diminutive (though occasionally it is an occupational name coming from the same Old French word, which means a hammer). The name Martinsmith, which looks occupational, is actually a corruption of the medieval Martinsmough, 'Martin's brother-in-law'. The same development is seen in Hudsmith (Hud's – i.e. Hugh's – brother-in-law), while the original form remains in Watmough, 'Walter's brother-in-law', and Hitchmough, 'Richard's brother-in-law'. Martinson or Martenson, as well as Martins or Martens, are also derivatives of Martin. In other languages the name appears as Martine, Martines, Martinez, Martineau, Martinelli, Martini, Martino and Martinuzzi.

The first name Martin appears in its Latinised form Martius in the Domesday Book records for 1066. However, the surname does not appear until a century later, the first mention being in the Red Book of the Exchequer for Cambridgeshire. Here in 1166 Walter and Helewis Martin are listed.

A MARTIN MISCELLANY

Martin brothers have on several occasions made major names for themselves in the decorative arts. In the eighteenth century Robert, Julien, Guilliaume and Étienne-Simon Martin invented and perfected the application of a special lacquer for furniture and furnishings. Known as *vernis-Martin*, this was extensively used at Versailles.

*

Admiral Sir William F. Martin was renowned in the Royal Navy for having his men arrested ('pinched') for even the slightest offence. Ever since, any Martin joining the Navy picks up the nickname 'Pincher'.

*

Simon Manfritie de Borton (1210–85) ascended the papal throne in 1281 calling himself Martin IV, under the mistaken assumption that there had already been Popes Martin II and III. His entire short reign was marred by similar ineptitudes, and he was driven from Rome by a popular uprising in 1285.

*

Glen Luther Martin (1886–1955) was a pioneer aviator and aircraft manufacturer. He made the first flight over the ocean, a short hop from Newport Beach to Santa Catalina Island. Later he formed a large aeroplane manufacturing company, which was responsible for producing such epoch-making craft as the B-26 bomber and the PBM Marina flying boat. Both of these played a major part in the World War II bombing of Germany.

*

Martins are members of the swallow family. The mud martin is so named because it makes its nest of sticks, straw and mud. Martens are weasel-like carnivores found in Canada, the northern US, Europe and the Far East. The soft, thick fur of these creatures is much valued.

*

In all, 8 towns in the United Kingdom are Martin-related. There are 17 in the United States including 5 Martins and 5 Martinsburgs. South Africa has a Martindale while New Zealand has a Martinborough. Because of the Saint Martin connections, related town and geographic names are widespread and notably prevalent in Latin-language areas.

*

With about 185,000 namesakes Martin is the 29th most popular surname in England and Wales. There are over 17,000 Martins in Scotland where it is 36th in popularity. In Ireland it is estimated that with about 15,000, Martin is the 38th most popular surname. The name is notably popular in and around Glasgow where an estimated one in about 269 families bears it. In descending numerical order Edinburgh, Nottingham and Leicester are other Martin strongholds. Around the world Martins are most popular in Canberra (one in 377 families), Ottawa (one in 417) and Sydney (one in 432). The United States counts Martins, Martinsons and Martinez's together – an estimated total of just over 1,179,000 makes this group their 8th most popular surname.

MILLER

RELATED NAMES

Other surnames which are related as to root, derivation or usage include:

Mellard	Millard	Millman	Millward
Meller	Millers	Mills	Millwood
Mellers	Millerson	Milne	Molineux
Millar	Millier	Milner	Mullard
	Muller	Mylne	

Not surprisingly, the surname Miller was originally an occupational name – for one who grinds (or mills) the corn. The earliest forms of this name are Mulnare (1275), Milner and Mylnere.

The original Milner, or Miller, has many related names. Common examples of these are Millward (the ward or keeper of the mill), Milne (usually meaning 'dweller or worker at the mill'), Millers (a derivative of Miller) and Millman.

There are also a number of names which would at first sight appear to be related to Miller, but come from completely different sources. Examples of these are Millican, Millikin (which derive from Milligan, which in turn comes from the Irish name Mulligan), and Millicent (which originates from a German first name meaning 'work-strong' and which came over to England with the Norman Conquest). Interestingly, Molineux, which looks at first sight to be from a different source, is a French name meaning 'miller' and is ultimately related to Miller by etymology.

The popular and widespread name Mills has two possible derivations, one of which is related to Miller. On the one hand it could be from 'dweller by the mills' (plural); on the other it could represent the first name Miles (now more common as Myles).

Owing to its early rural origins, the name Miller is extremely widespread, being one of the few English names which is common to all counties throughout the land. It is also the twentieth most popular Scottish name and, more surprisingly, was recently found to be sixth most popular in the United States – though many of these will have been anglicised from European versions of this occupational name or from similar-sounding more complex European names, or simply adopted by people whose names proved too long and/or too complex for everyday English use – as in many Polish or Greek names.

The name Miller began to appear early in the English records – though its earliest appearance was in a variation of the original Milner form. One John le Mulnare is mentioned in the Subsidy Rolls for Worcester for 1275. Only 21 years later the Miller form appeared in the Subsidy Rolls for Sussex, where one Ralf Muller is listed.

A MILLER MISCELLANY

Miss Marple and Hercule Poirot are the creations of Agatha Mary Miller (1891–1976), better known as Agatha Christie. Worldwide sales of her 77 detective novels are in the tens of millions. Dame Agatha is unique in being the only modern playwright to have had three West End plays running concurrently, including *The Mousetrap* which has run for a record-breaking 28 years.

*

Other Millers have also been notably successful as twentieth-century literary figures. Henry Miller (1891–1980) is famous for his sexually explicit novels *Tropic of Cancer* and *Tropic of Capricorn*, written and published in Paris and banned in the UK and US until the early Sixties. Arthur Miller (b.1915) is a major American dramatist whose best-known work *Death of A Salesman* won a 1949 Pulitzer Prize.

*

Famous English comedian Joseph Miller (1684–1738) was ironically dubbed 'The Father of Jests', since he was something of a dullard and the butt of contemporary jesters. A 'Joe Miller' was a popular nineteenth-century term synonymous with any joke, as in 'I don't see the Joe Miller of it'.

*

The most popular Allied band leader during World War II

was Glenn Miller (1904–44). The plane carrying him to entertain the troops at Christmas-time vanished over the sea and was never found. The 'Glenn Miller sound' goes on to this very day.

*

The United Kingdom has towns named Miller, Mill and Miller's Dale, South Africa has a Miller and Australia a Millaroo. The United States has 6 name-related towns while the Bahamas has a town called Millars and New Zealand has Miller's Flat and Millerton. Surprisingly few major rivers bear the name. Australia has a Miller river and a Miller's creek while the United States has a Millers falls.

*

With about 21,000 namesakes Miller is Scotland's 20th most popular surname. Thus about one out of every 240 Scots is named Miller. (The name is not common enough throughout England and Wales to be counted separately.) Miller is notably popular in and around Glasgow where an estimated one in about 206 families bears the name, and in Edinburgh where the figure is about one in 270. Around the world Millers are most common in Vancouver (one in 461 families), Canberra (one in 548), Toronto (one in 575) and Melbourne (one in 622). The United States has more Millers than the entire population of Birmingham – an estimated total of just over 1,190,000 makes this their 6th most popular surname.

MITCHELL

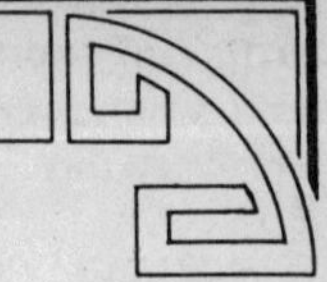

RELATED NAMES

Other surnames which are related as to root, derivation or usage include:

Meickle	Michel	Michison	Mitchel
Michael	Michelson	Mickle	Mitchelson
Michaels	Michie	Micklejohn	Mitchenson
Mitchinson	Mitchison	Mutch	

The surname Mitchell has two separate derivations. In the first it comes from the first name Michel, the Norman form of Michael. Michael is a name of great antiquity and comes from the Hebrew, where it means 'Who is God?'. The Archangel Michael appears in the Book of Revelations, where he overcomes Satan and the powers of evil. This rôle has made him the patron saint of soldiers. The first name Michael started to become popular in Europe around the twelfth century, probably as a result of its 'rediscovery' during the Crusades to the Holy Land. It has always been particularly popular in Ireland, to such an extent that it is now often used in the form of Mick, as a (fairly derogatory) nickname for an Irishman. Michael is presently one of the most popular first names in the United States.

The second derivation of Mitchell is as a nickname from the Middle English word 'muchel', (in the North, 'mickle') which means 'big', hence Micklejohn, 'big John'. The word survives today as 'much' in such place names as Much Haddington.

The original name Mitchell has many variations. Mitchel and Mitchelson are the most frequent, and Mitchenson and Mitchinson are both versions of Mitchelson. Other surnames from the same source are Michael and Michaels.

References to the name Michel began to appear in the records of the early thirteenth century. The earliest reference to it as a surname is in the Curia Regis Rolls for Northumberland. Here in 1205 the name Gilbert Michel is mentioned.

That example almost certainly comes from the first-name derivation.

A MITCHELL MISCELLANY

One of the greatest best-sellers of all times, *Gone With The Wind*, was written by Margaret Mitchell (1900–49). This romantic chronicle of the American Civil War sold over one million copies within six months of publication. The film version, starring Vivien Leigh as Scarlett O'Hara and Clark Cable as Rhett Butler, was for many years the longest movie ever released and has been seen by more people than any other film made.

*

The Scottish-born explorer Sir Thomas Livingstone Mitchell (1792–1855) began his adventurous career as an aide-de-camp to the Duke of Wellington in Spain. Later he explored uncharted regions of New South Wales in Australia, eventually laying out over 200 new towns and villages.

*

The many retail cooperatives throughout Britain and the US owe their existence to Lancashire-born John Thomas Whitehead Mitchell. He was the key figure in shaping the policies of the 1863 Cooperative Wholesale Society, basing the return of members' dividends on their total purchases. Radical Socialist Beatrice Webb later successfully championed his ideas.

*

Mitcheldean, Mitchell and Mitchel Troy are name-related towns in the United Kingdom. Canada and Australia each have one Mitchell while the United States has 4 such towns and Ireland has a Mitchelstown. There are 2 Mitchell rivers in Australia, one in Canada and 2 Mitchell lakes in the United States. Australia has a Mitchell Point.

*

With about 22,000 namesakes Mitchell is Scotland's 16th most popular surname. Thus about one out of every 230 Scots is named Mitchell. (The name is not common enough throughout England and Wales to be counted separately.) Mitchell is notably popular in and around Edinburgh where an estimated one in about 220 families bears the name, and in Glasgow where the figure is about one in 275. Around the world Mitchells are most common in Canberra (one in 500 families), Wellington (one in 542), Sydney (one in 631) and Melbourne (one in 639). The United States has more Mitchells than the entire population of Coventry – an estimated total of just over 390,000 makes this their 39th most popular surname.

MOORE

RELATED NAMES

Other surnames which are related as to root, derivation or usage include:

Atmore	Moorey	Moorman	Morecraft
Moor	Moorgate	Moors	Moreland
Moorcock	Moorhead	Moorwood	Moreman
Moorcroft	Moorhouse	Morcombe	Morland
Moorehead	Mooring	More	Morley
	Morton		

The surname Moore has two distinct derivations. In one it originated from the first name Moor, whose origins are of great antiquity. This comes from the Old French Maur, which in its turn derives from the Latin first name Maurus. (There was even a Saint Maurus in the sixth century.) The first name Maurus originally meant 'moor' (as in Othello the Moor) and was given to a native of North Africa. These were very rarely black people – like Othello – but were usually Arabs or Berbers. However, the name Maurus soon came to be used as a nickname for anyone with a dark complexion, meaning 'darkie' – almost certainly with much the same racialist undertones as the word 'darkie' has today. Thus this derivation of the name Moore came to England with the Normans in the eleventh century (see also Morris.)

The other derivation of the surname Moore is from the Anglo-Saxon word 'mōr' meaning 'heath'. It is thus a place name, being given to someone who lived at or on a moor, heath or fen. The earliest forms of the name were preceded by 'at' or 'de' (e.g. Harry at Moore) with the additional 'e' because of the dative case.

There are many names related to, or variations of, the original Moore. Common examples of these are Moorhouse (house or home in the fen or moor, also a frequent place name in the northern counties of England), Moorehead (dweller at the top edge, or head, of the moor, also local name from places in Northumbria and West Yorkshire), Moorcroft (croft, or cottage, on the moor), Moorman, Moorwood (dweller in or by the wood on the moor). The name Morton also derives from this source – being short for Moorton, meaning farm on the moor. However, two very similar names have different derivations. The surname Moorcock is sometimes derived from a diminutive of the first name More: Morcoc. However, it also derives on occasions from 'son of Maurice', or as a nickname from the bird, the moorcock. The name Moorson, more commonly Morson, comes from 'son of Morris'.

The name Moore is widespread throughout Britain and Ireland. However, in Ireland the name occasionally derives as an anglicised version of the Irish name O'More. This comes from the Irish Gaelic O'Mordha, which originates from the Gaelic first name 'Mordha' meaning 'majestic'.

The earliest mention of the surname Moore is in the 1185 Records of the Templars for Lincolnshire. Here one Johannes filius More is listed.

A MOORE MISCELLANY

Sir Thomas More (1478–1535) was a statesman, scholar, author – and finally a martyr. Today he is best remembered as the hero of the film *A Man for All Seasons*. This depicts his friendship with Henry VIII, and their final quarrel, when Thomas More refused to support Henry's divorce from Catherine of Aragon. For this Henry had him imprisoned, and later beheaded. Thomas More's saintliness of character soon became universally renowned. He was subsequently canonised by the Catholic Church while to this day there is a Thomas More room in the bounds of the Kremlin.

*

Several Moores have distinguished themselves in the arts of this century. One of the most notable of these is the Yorkshire sculptor Henry Moore (b.1898). A coal-miner's son, he is regarded by many as the world's greatest living sculptor. Another was America's greatest female poet of the twentieth century – Marianne Moore (1887–1972). Her many prizes included a Pulitzer, the National Book

Award, and the Gold Medal of the National Institute of Letters.

*

One of Britain's richest men is John Moores, the co-founder of the Liverpool-based pools firm of Littlewoods. Having left school at the age of 14 to work as a telephone operator his fortune is now estimated at around £850 million. Besides running his pools firm and a mail order business he is also a well-known benefactor of the arts. The prestigious annual 'Moores Exhibition' in Liverpool attracts entries from all Britain's greatest contemporary artists.

*

The United Kingdom has 19 Moore-related towns. These range from Moorby to Moortown (2). Jamaica has a Moore Town while Canada has a Moore's Mills and a Moores, and Australia a Moorlands and a Moorooka. In all, 21 US towns and cities relate to the name. Moore-related names for geographic features are common.

*

With about 137,000 namesakes Moore is the 33rd most popular surname in England and Wales. In Ireland it is estimated that with about 19,000, Moore is the 20th most popular surname. (The name is not common enough throughout Scotland to be counted separately.) Moore is notably popular in and around Leicester where an estimated one in about 255 families bears the name. In descending numerical order Coventry, Birmingham and Teesside are other Moore strongholds. Around the world Moores are most common in Canberra (one in 354 families), Sydney (one in 522) and Ottawa (one in 655). The United States has more Moores than the entire populations of Bristol and Nottingham combined – an estimated total of just under 728,000 makes this their 13th most popular surname.

MORGAN

RELATED NAMES

Other surnames which are related as to root, derivation or usage include:

Morgans Morganson Morganton Morgen

The surname Morgan is extremely ancient. Though it is known to be of Celtic origin, its meaning remains uncertain. The name itself derives from a Celtic first name which was rendered as Morcant in Old Breton, Old Welsh and Cornish; and as Morgunn in Pictish. One possible meaning of the name is 'sea-bright', in which case it would have been a nickname referring to the appearance or personality of its original holder.

The name Morgan is most frequently found in South Wales, where it is related to the Country of Glamorgan. Here the name was originally Ap-Morgan, meaning 'son of Morgan', (as in Ab-Evan, 'son of Evan', which became Bevan). However, the name also occurs often in Scotland, where it is known to have originated from Aberdeenshire and amongst the Mackays of Sutherland. There is even a Clan Morgan in Scotland and this clan title was used by the Mackays of the Reay country.

Other origins include ancient Brittany and Cornwall as well as England, where the name gave rise to the related Morgans, which is short for Morganson.

Morgan was the name of the early British monk who travelled to Europe and started the first Christian heresy. In Europe his name was Graecised to Pelagius – hence the Pelagian heresy, which denies original sin.

The surname Morgan appears in many forms in the early records. The earliest references are to the Latinised form Morganus, which occurs in the Pipe Rolls for Gloucestershire in 1159, and also in the Pipe Rolls for Salop in 1166. However, this form was probably used only for official records. The more vernacular form of Morgund is listed in Scottish records between 1204 and 1211. In 1214 the Curia Regis Rolls for Berkshire list a John Morgan.

A MORGAN MISCELLANY

The most notorious pirate of the Spanish Main was Sir Henry Morgan (1635–88). For over a decade he terrorised the Caribbean. Such was his power that at one time he commanded a fleet of 36 ships, with over 2,000 buccaneers, and at one stage actually seized control of Jamaica from the Spanish as well as Cuba. He later retired and died a respected planter in Jamaica.

*

Whimsical fairy Morgan le Fay is variously depicted in Arthurian romance as a magical healer, mistress of Avalon and later as a malign sorceress constantly plotting the death of Arthur and dreaming up evil schemes to discredit the Knights of the Round Table. As late as the nineteenth century the famous mirages seen in the Strait of Messina were popularly believed to be *Fata Morgana* (the Fairy Morgan) a name still used to describe them.

*

A morganatic marriage is one between a male of royal birth and a woman of lesser rank, with the provision that any children resulting from the union will not inherit their father's station or property.

*

Morgan horses, once the most popular breed in the US, are stylish, all-purpose steeds especially suited for riding. A horse named Justin Morgan (after its owner) was the early-nineteenth-century father of the breed with an eclectic pedigree that, among other strains, combined thoroughbreds and Arabians.

*

Morganite is a gem-like beryl prized for its lovely pink or rose-like colour.

*

Anglican clergyman William Morgan's 1588 translation of the Bible into Welsh became the written language taught to the

Welsh people for the next 200 years and thus standardised the language.

*

The United Kingdom has one name-related town, Morgan's Vale. Australia has a Morgan and a Morganville while Russia has a Morgana. In the US there are 15 name-related towns including the exotically designated Morganza. There are Morgan mountains in Australia and the US and a Morgan's Bluff in the Bahamas as well as a Morgan's Bay in South Africa and a Morgan Island in Antarctica.

*

With about 133,000 namesakes Morgan is the 37th most popular surname in England and Wales. (The name is not common enough throughout Scotland to be counted separately.) Morgan is notably popular in and around Cardiff where an estimated one in about 70 families bears the name. In descending numerical order Bristol, Coventry and Birmingham are other Morgan strongholds. Around the world Morgans are most common in Sydney (one in 821 families), Wellington (one in 893) and Auckland (one in 927). The United States has more Morgans than the entire population of Leicester – an estimated total of just under 287,000 makes this their 56th most popular surname.

MORRIS

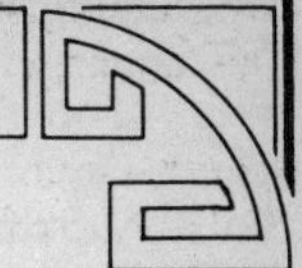

RELATED NAMES

Other surnames which are related as to root, derivation or usage include:

Fitzmaurice	Maurice	Morrice	Morrison
Fitzmorris	Morcock	Morrisey	Morriss
Marin	Morison	Morrish	Morrissey
	Morson	Morys	

The surname Morris is a variation of the name Maurice, which was, and still is, a popular first name. The first name Maurice came to England with the Norman Conquest and derives from the Old French name Meurisse. This name in turn came from the Latin first name Mauritius (like the island) which originates from the word Maurus, meaning a Moor (as in Othello the Moor, an inhabitant of North Africa, usually of Berber or Arab origin – see also Moore). Thus this name was originally given to a Moor. However, it was also often used as a nickname for anyone of swarthy or dark complexion.

The name Maurice spread all over Europe. There was even a St Maurice who was martyred in Switzerland in AD 286. (The fashionable ski resort of St Moritz is named after him.) When the name came to England, it gave itself to that most English of rural pastimes, the Morris Dance. Ironically, this originally meant 'Moorish Dance'.

The name Morris is found all over the land, but is most common in Wales, the Welsh border country and the southern counties of England. The variation Morrish is found in Somerset and Devon. This is a corruption of the more French Maurice, just as the French word liquorice is now often corrupted to liquorish. Other related names are Morrison (most common in the northern counties of England, and in Scotland), Morrice, and Fitzmaurice (son of Maurice).

The earliest mention of the surname Morris in the records

is of one Fulco Julius Mauricii (this being the Latin version of the name, with Julius meaning 'son of'). He appears in the records of the Templars for Lincolnshire in 1185. The slightly more recognisable Ricardus Julius Morys appears in the 1297 Subsidy Rolls for Yorkshire.

A MORRIS MISCELLANY

The English artist, poet and social reformer William Morris (1834–96) revolutionised Victorian taste with his designs for furniture, fabrics and wallpaper – which remain influential in interior design to this day.

*

A key figure in the development of the British motor industry was William Richard Morris (1877–1963), who later became Lord Nuffield. He started his business in a bicycle repair shop, and later set up his factory at Cowley, Oxford. The Morris Oxford car was his greatest popular success.

*

Liverpool-born American patriot Robert Morris was dubbed 'the Financier of the American Revolution' for his private rôle in procuring supplies and borrowing money to keep Washington's army going through the most crucial years of the revolution. Later he loyally served the fledgling nation by securing loans to help it through early financial crises. But by 1798 disastrous land speculations had eaten up his personal fortune, and he was arrested and clapped into a debtor's prison, where he stayed for 3½ years. After his release he died in obscurity, a broken man.

*

The sole name-related town in the United Kingdom is Morriston while Canada has a Morris and a Morrisburg. A total of 24 United States towns and cities are Morris-related. Name-related geographic features are rare. Australia has a Morris mountain and there is a Morris Island off the coast of South Carolina in the United States.

*

With about 153,000 namesakes Morris is the 28th most popular surname in England and Wales. There are over 22,000 Morrisons in Scotland, where this variation is 18th in popularity. Morris is notably popular in and around Cardiff where an estimated one in about 215 families bears the name. In descending numerical order Birmingham, Coventry and Liverpool are other Morris strongholds. Around the world Morris's and Morrisons are most common in Wellington (one in 435 families), Auckland (one in 442) and Vancouver (one in 485). The United States has more Morris's and Morrisons than the entire population of Bristol – in combination an estimated total of just under 478,000 makes this their 27th most popular surname.

MURPHY

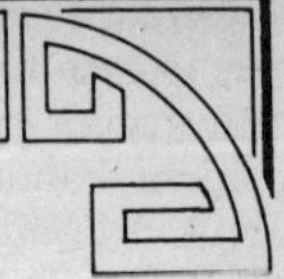

RELATED NAMES

Other surnames which are related as to root, derivation or usage include:

MacMurphy Morchoe Morphey Murphey
O'Morchoe O'Murphy

The name Murphy is easily the most widely held surname in Ireland and as such appears in large numbers wherever Irishmen have emigrated. It has also long been found in Scotland, but it is not indigenous there, its presence being due solely to early immigration.

There were three original family clans (or septs) of this name, in Wexford, Roscommon and Cork, where there are still more Murphys per head of population than anywhere else. Once upon a time the forms MacMurphy and O'Murphy (both meaning 'son of Murphy') were widespread, but the prefixes have generally been dropped. The MacMurphys were originally found mainly in Armagh and Tyrone.

The name Murphy came from the Irish Gaelic O'Murchadha which derives from the first name Murchadh, meaning 'sea warrior'. It is thus possible that some, but certainly not all, of the original Murphys may have been of Viking origin.

An early form of the name Murphy is Morchoe (or O'Morchoe). This is still in use, and the chief of the O'Murphys is called O'Morchoe.

Unlike most names derived from the Gaelic, Murphy has few variants. The alternative spelling Murphey is still found, but it is in no way as popular as Murphy.

The name Murphy does not appear in early English records, and the name did not come to England in any significant numbers until the great Irish immigration of the eighteenth century.

A MURPHY MISCELLANY

In 1952 amateur hypnotist Morey Bernstein put a young

housewife Virginia Tighe (b.1923) into a deep trance. Thus began one of the strangest controversies of the century. Tighe proceeded to recount in great detail her former life as an Irishwoman named Bridey Murphy, born in Cork in 1798. She supplied details of that time and place no modern young American could be expected to know, such as slang expressions and the title of a book which, it turned out, had been published in Ireland but not in the US. Bernstein's account of his experiment, *The Search for Bridey Murphy*, instantly became a best-seller, with 170,500 copies in print within two months. However, *Life* magazine, through its own investigations, revealed that in childhood one of Mrs Tighe's neighbours had been a Mrs Corkell, maiden name Bridey Murphy. That revelation, plus other inconsistencies in Bridey's recollections, cooled the public's interest but the episode raised questions that have yet to be satisfactorily answered.

*

Murphys have made a major impact on medicine. American doctor William Murphy shared a Nobel Prize with two others for his discovery that raw liver cured pernicious anaemia, while American surgeon John Benjamin Murphy was a pioneer in the study and treatment of peritonitis, and invented the Murphy Button (1892), a device for linking severed intestinal ends thus enabling important advances in gastrointestinal surgery. Artificial lung collapse (by the injection of nitrogen, instrumental in the treatment of tuberculosis) was another Murphy innovation.

*

Marie Louise Murphy (1733–1814) rose from being a draper's daughter to become Louis XV's mistress. Madame de Pompadour stage-managed the whole affair by arranging to have the King meet Marie Louise while she posed at Versailles as the Virgin for a portrait of the Holy Family. When the king tired of her she was replaced in his affections by her sister, Marie Brigette.

*

Irish-born Arthur Murphy was an eighteenth-century all-rounder. As publisher of the *Gray's Inn Journal* he got to know Dr Johnson, later writing an *Essay on Johnson.* When he encountered financial reverses he took to the stage, so successfully that he was able to pay off his debts; then he began to both write and produce plays on his own. After entering Lincoln's Inn in 1757 he was called to the Bar and practised law successfully while finding time to publish a highly regarded translation of Tacitus.

*

Few related place and major geographical feature names attach to Murphy. The United States has 3 towns called Murphy, one Murphys, and one Murphysboro as well as a Murphy Lake, while Antarctica has a Mount Murphy.

*

With about 10,000 namesakes Murphy is Scotland's 72nd most popular surname. Thus about one out of every 510 Scots is named Murphy. In Ireland about 66,000 Murphys make this the country's most popular surname. (The name is not common enough throughout England and Wales to be counted separately.) Around the world Murphys are most common in Canberra (one in 605 families), Ottawa (one in 655), Sydney (one in 694) and Brisbane (one in 801). The United States has more Murphys than the entire population of Newcastle – an estimated total of just over 327,000 makes this their 51st most popular surname.

MURRAY

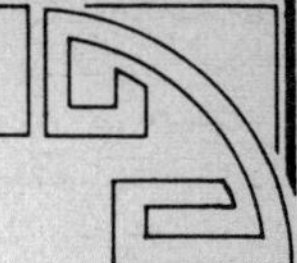

RELATED NAMES

Other surnames which are related as to root, derivation or usage include:

Kilmorey	MacMurray	Morrey	Murrey
MacGilmore	Merry	Morrie	Murrie
MacIlmurray	Moray	Murie	Murrihy
	Murry	O'Murry	

The surname Murray is a place name deriving from the county of Moray (as in Moray Firth) in Scotland. As such it is a Scots Gaelic derivation from the ancient British place name, whose exact meaning remains unknown. It is also the English spelling for a wide variety of Irish surnames ranging from O'Muirighte to Mac Gille Mhuire.

The Irish Murrays are mainly in the north, and their presence is due almost entirely to the Cromwellian land settlements and other immigrations from Scotland.

A witness to the Royal Charter to the Abbey of Holyrood in 1203 was one William de Moravia – the first Murray on record. The Moray (or Murray) origin of this name is confirmed by the appearance in the records 50 years later of one Malcolm de Moravia, who witnessed a charter by the Earl of Strathern.

Some modern Murrays living in England may well have a different origin. These almost certainly derive from the Middle English name Murie (more recognisable in its root form Merry). This was originally a nickname, describing an obvious quality of character. These Murrays are sometimes spelt Murrie. Other widespread variations on Murray include Murrey, Morrey and Murry.

A MURRAY MISCELLANY

The Murray Fracture Zone is a long submarine mountain range stretching nearly 2,000 miles across the Pacific Ocean from northern Hawaii to the shores of south-western California.

It is named after Sir John Murray (1841–1914), the Ottawa-born pioneer in the science of oceanography.

*

One of the most influential English literary figures in the early decades of this century was John Middleton Murry. His close and often stormy relationship with the novelist D.H. Lawrence was depicted in thinly disguised form in Lawrence's novel *Women in Love*, which was later made into a controversial film by the flamboyant film director Ken Russell.

*

Australia's principal river is the Murray River. It flows through some 1,000 miles of south-eastern Australia and was named after the Colonial Secretary, Sir George Murray. The Murray Valley is the main wheat-growing and sheep-farming area in south-western Australia. This valley also has a disease named after it, Murray Valley encephalitis, a form of brain tissue inflammation which was once prevalent in the area. The disease is also known as Australian X disease, and is transmitted by bird migration.

*

The American astronomer Bruce Murray masterminded the data-finding equipment for the Mariner 10 space rocket which provided us with revolutionary new knowledge about the planet Mercury.

*

There are no name-related towns or major geographic features in the United Kingdom. Both Canada and the US have Murrayvilles while the US also has 4 towns called Murray and a Murray City. Australia has a Murray Downs and a Murrysboro, while Bermuda has a Murray's Anchorage. Murray rivers are common outside of the United Kingdom while Australia's Murray range and the Pacific Ocean's Murray Deep are world famous.

*

With about 27,000 namesakes Murray is Scotland's 12th most popular surname. Thus about one out of every 195 Scots is named Murray. In Ireland about 20,000 Murrays make this the country's 18th most popular surname. (The name is not common enough throughout England and Wales to be counted separately.) Murray is notably popular in and around Glasgow where an estimated one in about 190 families bears the name. Around the world Murrays are most common in Canberra (one in 622 families), Sydney (one in 686), Auckland (one in 752) and Ottawa (one in 819). The United States has more Murrays than the entire population of Brighton – an estimated total of just under 194,000 makes this their 106th most popular surname.

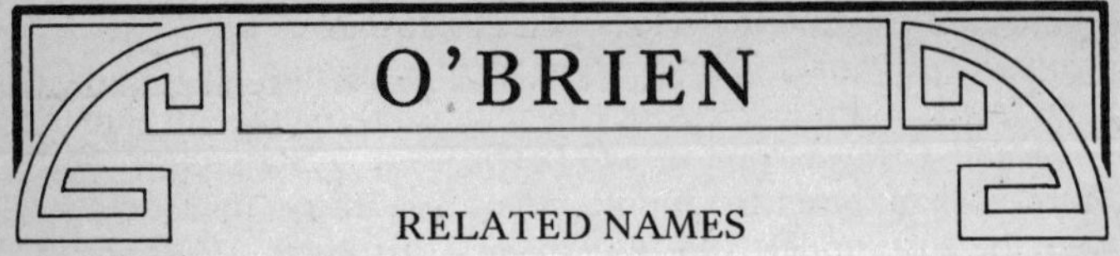

O'BRIEN

RELATED NAMES

Other surnames which are related as to root, derivation or usage include:

Brian	Bryan	O'Briain	O'Bryan
Brien	Bryant	O'Brian	O'Bryen

The surname O'Brian comes from the Irish Gaelic O'Briain, which means 'son of Brian'. Brian is an ancient Celtic name of uncertain origin – but the most likely explanation is that it means 'hill'.

The family clans of the O'Brians have great importance in Ireland. This is mainly due to their illustrious predecessor, the great Brian Born, King of Leinster and Munster, who fought the Vikings at the Battle of Clontarf.

The O'Brians were originally found mainly in Munster, but are now numerous all over Ireland, and indeed wherever Irishmen have immigrated. It is not unexpected to find the name O'Brian occurring frequently in London, Boston, or Sydney, but a little-known fact is that one of the great wines of France – Chateau Haut Brian – is in fact derived from the Irish O'Brian. (The O'Brians are not the only Irish to have distinguished themselves in this most French of preserves – witness the Hennessys of Cognac fame.)

In some cases the Irish O'Brian is derived from O'Byrne (see Byrne), derived from O'Biorain. Also, during the centuries of British persecution in Ireland, many Irish O'Brians found it prudent to anglicise their name to Byran, Bryon or Bryom: compare the case of the Byrnes, above. In other cases it is a derivation of the first name Brian, which in this instance came to England with the Norman Conquest, being found in Latinised form in the Domesday Book, and giving rise to a number of variant English surnames such as Bryant and Byrne. Thus the Irish who switched from O'Brian to Bryan were really doing little more than completing a circle of variations.

AN O'BRIEN MISCELLANY

The O'Briens have produced several Irish literary figures during this century. The novelist Edna O'Brien (b. 1932) is famed for her romantic portrayals of her childhood in remote County Clare. The humorist Flann O'Brien (1911–66), whose real name was Brian O'Nolan, is best remembered for his hilarious novel *At Swim-Two-Birds.* Conor Cruise O'Brien (b. 1917) is a politician and journalist, as well as a biographer. He served as UN representative in the Congo during the Katanga crisis, and is now editor of the *Observer.*

*

Special effects genius Willis O'Brien gave birth to one of the screen's greatest stars, King Kong. His brilliant stop-animation techniques reached a peak with the climactic battle with aircraft atop the Empire State Building – one of the most memorable scenes in cinema history. O'Brien's handiwork was unsurpassed 43 years later, when Dino De Laurentiis, employing the latest technology, resurrected the giant ape. A laudable attempt, the second ape wasn't a patch on the strangely charming original.

*

Place and major geographic feature names related to O'Brien are rare. The United Kingdom has none. Ireland has 2 towns – O'Briensbridge and O'Briens Town, while Canada has one town called simply O'Brien.

*

With about 35,000 namesakes O'Brien is Ireland's 6th most popular surname. Thus about one out of every 135 residents of Ireland is an O'Brien. (The name is not common enough throughout England, Scotland and Wales to be counted separately.) Around the world O'Briens are most common in Canberra (one in 500 families), Melbourne (one in 785) and Brisbane (one in 887). The United States has an estimated total of just under 133,000 O'Briens – this makes it their 195th most popular surname.

O'NEILL

RELATED NAMES

Other surnames which are related as to root, derivation or usage include:

McNeal	Neale	Nelson	Nigel
NcNeil	Neel	Niall	Nihill
McNell	Neill	Nielsen	Niles
Neal	Nell	Nielson	O'Neil

The surname O'Neil comes from the Irish Gaelic, which is spelt the same. It means 'son or descendant of Neil (or Neal)'. This first name was originally Nial, and came from the Old Irish 'niadh', meaning 'champion'.

This first name has been popular in Ireland since earliest times. During the Viking invasions its popularity spread throughout the Norse world. In Iceland it became Njal (as seen in *The Story of Burnt Njal*), and in France it became Nel (or Nele). Here it was later Latinised to Nigellus (meaning 'black') which gave over to the variant Nigel.

Various forms of the name appear as a first name in the Domesday Book. Consequently, it soon gave rise to many variant surnames – such as Nelson and Nielson (which developed on its own in Scandinavian from the same first-name source).

The main family clan of the Irish O'Neills are the illustrious O'Neills of Ulster. Here they originated in Tyrone, being descended from the legendary Niall of the Nine Hostages. Other family clans originated further south in Waterford and Carlow– though the name still remains most numerous in the Ulster counties of Tyrone, Antrim and Down. It is Ireland's tenth most popular name.

Widespread variations on the surname O'Neill range from Neal to Niles, and from Nihill to Nigel. Again, these are largely of Norman origin.

The first mention of any surname related to O'Neill appears

in the Domesday Book records for Berkshire in 1086, where one Willelmus filius Nigelli is listed. After this many variations appear in England, but it is unlikely that any of these are of Irish origin until the eighteenth century or even later.

AN O'NEILL MISCELLANY

Shane's Castle, perched on County Antrim's Lough Neagh, is the ancient stronghold of the O'Neill clan. Thirty feet up the main tower's south wall there is a sculpture known as the Black Head of the O'Neills. According to ancient legend, the family will come to a tragic end if the head is ever destroyed. The O'Neills also have a banshee in the form of a beautiful young woman who paces back and forth wringing her hands and singing a haunting lament. Her appearance is said to herald the death of any member of the family unlucky enough to hear her wailing.

*

The internationally known US physicist, Gerard K. O'Neill, has already started work on an idea long popular with science fiction writers, the colonisation of outer space. In 1969 he set out to discredit the possibility in a seminar, discovered it was actually a viable proposition, and convinced NASA, which awarded him a grant in 1975 to pursue the idea.

*

Hugh O'Neill (c. 1540–1616), the second Earl of Tyrone, was an Irish rebel. Known in his time as 'The Great Earl', he led several Roman Catholic uprisings against English rule. Confirmed in his title by James I but under threat of arrest because of a dispute over lands, he fled to Europe in 1607 in an unsuccessful attempt to raise an army. This 'flight of the earls', as it is known, marked the end of Gaelic Ulster, which was then anglicised.

*

The iconoclastic English educator, A.S. Neill (1883–1973), established the experimental boarding school, Summerhill, in the early 1920s. His ideas on liberal education have considerably influenced subsequent development in education at all levels.

*

Towns and major geographic features which relate to O'Neill

are extremely rare. The United States has one – O'Neill, Nebraska.

*

With about 31,000 namesakes O'Neill is Ireland's 10th most popular surname. Thus about one out of every 155 residents of Ireland is an O'Neill. (The name is not common enough throughout England, Scotland and Wales to be counted separately.) Around the world O'Neills are most common in Canberra (one in 1,150 families), Sydney (one in 1,575) and Ottawa (one in 1,637). The United States has an estimated total of just over 56,000 O'Neills – making this their 519th most popular surname.

PARKER

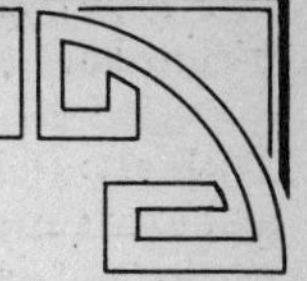

RELATED NAMES

Other surnames which are related as to root, derivation or usage include:

Duparc	Parke	Parkes	Parkhouse
Park	Parkerhouse	Parkhill	Parkhurst
	Parkman	Parks	

Parker is an ancient occupational name. It probably first came to this country with the Norman Conquest, though it possibly existed here prior to 1066. The surname Parker derives from the Old French word 'parquer' ('parchier'), which means 'park keeper' or 'ranger'. The Old French word derives in turn from a Germanic original meaning 'a park, enclosure, or thinly wooded land kept for beasts of the chase'.

There are several related surnames, such as Parkman, and Parkhouse (place name for a dweller in a house in a park), and Duparc (Norman, meaning 'of the park').

Variations on the name Parker include Park, Parke, Parks and Parkes. Park and Parkes are, strictly speaking, place names (i.e. a dweller in a park). However, as often as not they probably indicated someone who worked in a park, and were thus occupational names.

The first reference to the surname Parker is in the Domesday Book records for Somerset where, in 1086, one Anschetel Parcher is listed.

A PARKER MISCELLANY

When someone can't mind his own business, he's colloquially labelled a 'nosey parker'. The original was sixteenth-century English clergyman Matthew Parker, Archbishop of Canterbury under Queen Elizabeth I, whose critics dubbed him 'Nosey Parker' because he kept poking his nose into church matters that weren't his concern.

*

One man stood between Abraham Lincoln and assassin John Wilkes Booth – an alcoholic policeman named John Parker, the only guard posted outside the President's box at Ford's Theater. Half-way through the evening's performance he wandered off to get a drink, with consequences that changed the course of American history.

*

Comanche leader Quanah Parker, son of a chief who had married a white woman captured in childhood, led a year-long Texas rebellion of 700 warriors against the full might of the US cavalry before agreeing to settle on a reservation in 1875. He went on to become a powerful mediator between his people and the whites, spending his last 30 years as a successful businessman while still retaining his Indian culture and beliefs.

*

British Admiral Sir Hyde Parker sent a withdrawal signal to the Baltic Fleet during the 1801 Battle of Copenhagen. His subordinate, Horatio Nelson, whose small ships had done most of the fighting, put his telescope to his blind eye so he could honestly claim he hadn't received the order, then went on to win the battle.

*

Scottish explorer Mungo Park (1771–1806) was the first European to explore the Niger and several other interior regions of Africa.

*

The United Kingdom has no towns or major geographic features which are related to the name Parker. Canada has a town called Parkerview while the United States has 10 related-name towns and cities (including 5 called Parker) as well as the famous Parker Dam. Australia has a Parker hill, a Parker range and Parker Point while Hong Kong has a Parker mountain.

*

With about 117,000 namesakes Parker is the 49th most popular surname in England and Wales. (The surname is not common enough throughout Scotland to be counted separately.) Parker is notably popular in and around Leeds where an estimated one in about 365 families bears the name. In descending numerical order Nottingham, Leicester and Bradford are other Parker strongholds. Around the world Parkers are most common in Sydney (one in 852 families), Wellington (one in 893) and Melbourne (one in 953). The United States has more Parkers than the entire population of Newcastle – an estimated total of just under 339,000 makes this their 49th most popular surname.

PATTERSON

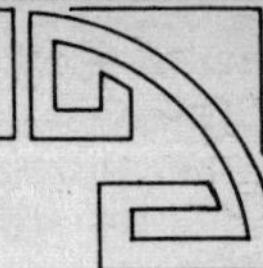

RELATED NAMES

Other surnames which are related as to root, derivation or usage include:

Fitzpatrick	Paterson	Patrick	Pattinson
Pater	Paton	Patricks	Pattison
		Patton	

The surname Patterson derives from a first name and means 'son of Patrick'. The first name Patrick has a long history and goes back to Roman times, where it comes from the Latin word 'patricus', meaning 'nobleman'. The word 'patrician' comes from the same source, and the popular girl's name Patricia is the feminine form.

The popularity of the first name Patrick in this country originated largely from the fifth-century saint of the same name. St Patrick almost certainly came originally from Scotland, but he is famous mainly for having brought Christianity to Ireland. For this deed he is now patron saint of Ireland, and his name is easily the most popular first name there. The diminutive of the name has even become the vernacular nickname for an Irishman – Paddy.

In Scotland, the first name Patrick became synonymous for a while with Peter, and it may well be that some Scottish Pattersons originate from this other first name (Peter comes from the Greek 'petros' meaning 'rock'). Scotland also tends to spell Patterson differently from the English form. The English form almost invariably has two t's.

There are several variant surnames arising from the same original source as Patterson. The best known of these are Pattison (the form used south of the Scottish border, especially in Cumbria and Westmorland), Patton and Paton (which are from a double diminutive of Patrick, with an added Old French suffix), and the obvious Patrick.

The origins of the surname Patterson become much more apparent in the early versions found in the records – one of the earliest of which is William Patrison. He is mentioned in the 1446 records for Aberdeen.

A PATTERSON MISCELLANY

Australian poet Andrew 'Old Banjo' Paterson made a memorable contribution to the nation when 'Waltzing Matilda' appeared in a 1917 collection of his verse. Set to music, it quickly became Australia's unofficial anthem.

*

Liberal penologist Sir Alexander Paterson emphasised the rehabilitative aspects of England's Borstal system of reformatories. He felt that it was the system's job to spark a desire for reform within the offender, rather than try to impose it, and humanised institutions for 16- to 21-year-olds by introducing the revolutionary house system, in which groups of inmates live together with a permanent housemaster and staff. He also promoted interesting work schemes, extended education and a vigorous sports programme.

*

Scots-born stone-cutter Robert Paterson (1715–1801) earned his nickname 'Old Mortality' when he abandoned his wife and five children to devote forty years to the task of repairing and erecting headstones to martyrs.

*

South African novelist Alan Paton was an early protester against the iniquities of apartheid. His best-selling *Cry the Beloved Country* (1948) was a moving examination of his homeland's racial problems.

*

Financier William Paterson founded the Bank of England in 1694. King William III approved his plan for a national bank when merchants raised £1,200,000 from shareholders and loaned it to the King at 8 per cent interest. William then granted the Bank a Royal Charter.

*

General George Smith Patton (1885–1945) was the hell-for-leather commander of the US 3rd Army which drove the Nazis back across France in 1944.

*

The only related place name in the United Kingdom is Patterdale in Cumbria. South Africa has one town called Patersen, the United States has 2, along with 5 Pattersons and one Pattisen. Australia has a Patersen river and a Patersen range while mountains in Canada's Yukon and in California are named Patterson. New Zealand has a Patterson Inlet while the New Hebrides has a Pattersen Passage.

*

With about 21,000 namesakes Paterson is Scotland's 22nd most popular surname. Thus about one out of every 250 Scots is named Paterson. (The name is not common enough throughout England and Wales to be counted separately.) Paterson is notably popular in and around Edinburgh where an estimated one in about 225 families bears the name, and in Glasgow where the figure is about one in 240. Around the world Patersons are most common in Wellington (one in 723 families), Auckland (one in 773) and Vancouver (one in 865). The United States tallies Patersons and Pattersons together – an estimated combined total of just over 207,000 makes this their 95th most popular surname.

PHILLIPS

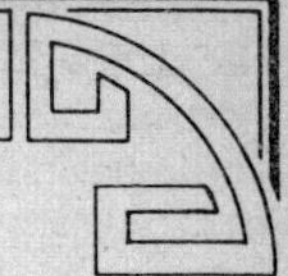

RELATED NAMES

Other surnames which are related as to root, derivation or usage include:

Filkin	Philcox	Phillipson	Philps
Fill	Philip	Phillpot	Philson
Filpot	Philips	Philp	Phips
Phelps	Philipson	Philpot	Phipps
Philbin	Phillip	Philpott	Piaf
Potkin	Pott	Pottell	

The surname Phillips derives from the first name Philip. The 's' is short for 'son', so strictly speaking Phillips means 'son of Philip'.

The first name Philip comes from the Ancient Greek and means 'lover of horses'. (The prefix 'phil-' means 'lover of', as in philosophy (lover of wisdom) and philanthropy (lover of one's fellow men)). The first name Philip achieved wide popularity throughout Christendom owing to the apostle Philip. However, this first name rapidly went out of fashion in England during the reign of Elizabeth I, when our national enemy was Spain. In those days the King of Spain was Philip II, and with England under the threat of the Armada the name Philip became about as popular in England as Adolf is at present. The first name Philip remained under a cloud for several centuries after this, and did not really revive in popularity until the start of the reign of the second Queen Elizabeth, the popularity of the Queen's husband causing the name to come into fashion again. Prince Philip, being descended from the Greek royal family, was named after European royalty, where the name has always been popular.

The surname Philip (or Phillips), on the other hand, did not suffer such dramatic changes in fortune. Phillips, like any name derived from a widespread first name, has a whole host of related names (compare the surnames for Robert, David and John). The surname Phelps (originally as Philps) derives from an abbreviated form of Philip, as does the more obvious but rarer Philson. Phipps is the same. Philpot (and thus Filpot) derives from the once popular diminutive, Philip-ot, a French diminutive form. (In this way Mary gives us the name Marriot, and nowadays in France Charlie Chaplin ('Charlie') is still commonly known as 'Charlot').

Other derivative surnames from the first name Philip include Fill, Filkin, and Philcox. In some cases even the original first syllable has been dropped, thus we get (by way of Philpot) the surnames Pott, Potkin, and Pottell – though in some cases these surnames have alternative entirely separate derivations.

The first name Philip first arrived in England during the twelfth century, coming by way of France in the French form Philippe. From this time on it appears regularly in the records as a first name. The earliest reference to the surname comes in the 1275 Hundred Rolls for Norfolk, where one Henry Philip is listed.

A PHILLIPS MISCELLANY

Tuberculosis was one of the scourges of the nineteenth century. The Scottish physician Sir Robert William Phillip played a major role in its prevention and cure, and founded Europe's first TB dispensary at Edinburgh in 1887. By the time of his death in 1939, the dread disease had been brought under control.

*

The Phillips Curve, named after A.W. Phillips, is a graphic representation of the economic relationship between the rate of unemployment and the rate of change of wages. It indicates that wages tend to rise faster when unemployment is low.

*

The Phillips Collection is a small but outstanding collection of late-nineteenth- and early-twentieth-century American and European paintings. The museum, in Washington DC, was founded in 1918 by Duncan Phillips.

*

In 1891 Anton Frederik Philips founded Philips Electric in Holland, now one of the world's largest firms for the manufacture of electrical appliances and lighting equipment.

*

In 1687 the English colonial administrator Sir William Phipps (1651–95) headed an expedition to the Caribbean in search of sunken treasure and came back with £300,000 of Spanish gold. With his newfound wealth he bought himself a knighthood, and eventually rose to become Royal Governor of Massachusetts. He was later recalled to England, however, to face charges of misgovernment, but died before his trial.

*

The United Kingdom has no towns or major geographic features which are related to this name but Phillips's need not feel downhearted. An entire country is their namesake – the Philippines. Canada has a Philipsburg, South Africa a Philipstown and a Philippolis, Belgium a Philipville, Holland a Phillippine and West Germany a Philippsburg. Some 14 United States towns and cities are Phillips-related. Geographic features with the name are common and include Australia's famed Phillips range.

*

With about 131,000 namesakes Phillips is the 38th most popular surname in England and Wales. (The name is not common enough throughout Scotland to be counted separately.) Phillips is notably popular in and around Cardiff where an estimated one in about 150 families bears the name. In descending numerical order Bristol, Birmingham and Coventry are other Phillips strongholds. Around the world Phillips's are most common in Wellington (one in 652 families), Canberra (one in 657) and Melbourne (one in 707). The United States has more Phillips's than the entire population of Coventry – an estimated total of just under 380,000 makes this their 40th most popular surname.

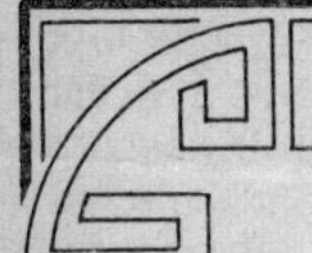

PRICE

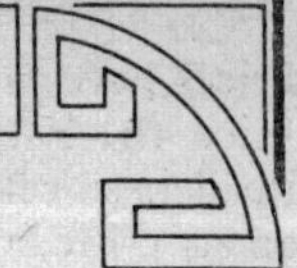

RELATED NAMES

Other names which are related as to root, derivation or usage include:

Prise Pryce Pryse Rees
Reese Rhys Rice

The surname Price originated in Wales. It is a corruption of the name Ap-rhys, meaning 'son of Rhys'. Another similarly derived Welsh name is Bevan, which comes from a corruption of Ab-Evan. Rice is better known in the form Rees or Rhys, and the first name Rhys is thought to derive from the Old Welsh, meaning 'ardour'.

The surname Price is found all over Wales and in the Welsh border counties, as are the previously mentioned names to which it is clearly related.

Occasionally, the surname Price has an English origin. The word 'pris' came to England with William the Conqueror and the Normans in 1066, then, as a word for the price of goods, in the thirteenth century it became an occupational name given to a pricer or fixer of prices (with 'fixer' in the original sense of the word – no deviousness is implied).

Popular variations on this name are Pryce, Prise, and Pryse. It is also often found in double-barrelled form with the widespread Welsh names Jones and Thomas, as in Price-Jones and Price-Thomas. The surname Thomas derives from the first name, which comes from the Ancient Aramaic word meaning 'twin' (for further details see Thomas). The surname Jones is short for 'son of John'. The first name John comes from the Hebrew meaning 'God is gracious' (see Johnson).

The first mention of the Welsh form of Price comes in the 1393 Archives for the City of London, where one Jorwerth ap Reys is listed. However, the Anglo-Norman name appears even earlier, in the 1297 Accounts for the County of Cornwall, where one Robert Price is mentioned.

A PRICE MISCELLANY

Prices have made a name for themselves in the arts. Vincent Price (b. 1911) has been a superstar of horror movies and thrillers since the early Thirties. He also has a second career as an art critic, and owns a remarkable collection of Impressionist paintings. Leontine Price (b. 1927) is the first black American soprano to achieve superstar status in the world of international opera. Her appearance in the 1950's revival of *Porgy and Bess* is now remembered as a classic. English character actor Dennis Price has appeared in such notable films as *Kind Hearts and Coronets* and *I'm All Right, Jack* and his greatest recent role was as the unflappable Jeeves in *The World of Wooster.* In fact, Dennis Price's real name is Dennistown Franklyn.

*

One of the great master-buildings designed by America's greatest twentieth-century architect, Frank Lloyd Wright (1868–1959), is the Price Tower in Bartlesville, Oklahoma. It was erected in 1956 and incorporates many of his revolutionary 'organic' ideas.

*

The National Laboratory of Psychical Research was founded in 1937 by Harry Price. He advertised in *The Times* for objective observers to witness psychical phenomena. Countless inexplicable 'phenomena' have been, and continue to be, investigated by this society, though their authenticity continues to be doubted by the sceptical.

*

The early American architect Bruce Price designed some of North America's most distinctive buildings. His most memorable works include the imposing Gothic-style Chateau Frontenac hotel in Quebec City, Montreal's Royal Victoria College, and several dormitories at Yale University. He also laid out New York's Tuxedo Park, and designed many of the houses there.

*

Bonamy Price, professor of political economy at Oxford in the late nineteenth century, helped mould economic thinking of the day in books such as *The Principles of Currency* and *Chapters on Practical Political Economy.*

*

The United Kingdom has one name-related place – Price Town, while Canada has one town called Price and the United States has 3 so named as well as a Pricetown. Australia and the United States have Price rivers, while Canada boasts a Price Island in British Columbia.

*

With about 109,000 namesakes Price is the 48th most popular surname in England and Wales. (The name is not common enough throughout Scotland to be counted separately.) Price is notably popular in and around Cardiff where an estimated one in about 140 families bears the name. In descending numerical order Birmingham, Liverpool and Bristol are other Price strongholds. Around the world Prices are most common in Canberra (one in 1,045 families), Wellington (one in 1,168) and Sydney (one in 1,283). The United States has more Prices than the entire population of Southampton – an estimated total of just over 237,000 makes this their 81st most popular surname.

RELATED NAMES

Other surnames which are related as to root, derivation or usage include:

Reade	Red	Reed	Reide
Reader	Redd	Reede	Reidy
Readett	Rede	Reeder	Ridding
Reading	Reditt	Reedman	Riding
Readman	Redman	Reeds	Rufus

These surnames have two distinct origins. The most usual derivation is from the nickname 'reed' or 'rede', which is Middle English for red. Thus the name would be given to someone with a ruddy complexion or red hair. This latter fact, together with its prevalence in East Anglia, the north-eastern counties of England, and Scotland (where it is spelt Reid), suggests that some of the original holders of this name were of Norse origin – though the name has long been widespread throughout the land.

The Old English word 'read' – 'red', also occurs in some place names, as perhaps in the Cumberland Redmayne which might mean 'red stone'. It appears as a personal name Reāda – 'the red one', in Reading (Berkshire), 'the place where the people called after Reāda live'. But not all examples of Reading as a surname necessarily allude to the Berkshire surname. Some may derive from places called Reading (in Kent), Reddings (Worcestershire), Redding Wood (Herefordshire), and so on. There was an Old English word 'ried' – 'a clearing', giving rise to place names Read and Reed, from which some surnames would be derived.

Finally, there is a third possible origin, an Old English word 'hreod' – 'reed', which gives us the place names Readett, Reditt etc. – 'reed-bed', and the occupational surnames Reader, Reeder, Readman, Reedman, and Redman – 'reed-man, reed-cutter, thatcher'.

The surname Read is one of the oldest in the records. The first mention of the nickname derivation appears before the Norman Conquest in the earliest Kent annals. Here Leofwine se Reade is mentioned in the records for 1016–20. After the Norman Conquest, this form of Read (and sometimes the alternative variation) often became Latinised to Rufus (as in William Rufus, William the Conqueror's son).

The earliest mention of the place-name derivation is in the 1160 records for Sussex where one Alwin de Larede is mentioned.

A REID MISCELLANY

Reids have made a notable contribution to the fine arts on two continents. Sir George Reid, Scottish landscape and portrait painter, headed the Royal Scottish Academy during 1891–1902. His paintings hang in museums in London, Edinburgh, Oxford, Aberdeen, Glasgow, Liverpool and Manchester. He is also noted for his book illustrations. Canadian George Andrew Reid's career was remarkably similar. Born in Canada in 1860, he served as president of his country's Royal Academy and later headed the Ontario College of Art.

*

Henry Fielding Reid was an American seismologist who developed the 'elastic rebound' theory explaining earthquake mechanics (1911).

*

Down-to-earth eighteenth-century philosopher Thomas Reid displayed one of the Scotsman's most basic qualities when he opposed the empirical scepticism of Locke and Hume with his 'philosophy of common sense'. His approach accepted the existence of things and didn't try to make subjective mental phenomena of them. Similarly, his system's morality was based on an intuitive perception of ethics. Such views led to professorships at both Aberdeen and Glasgow.

*

American army physician Walter Reed (1861–1902) conducted decisive experiments that proved typhoid germs are transmitted by the mosquito. His findings led to the elimination of yellow fever in Havana during the Spanish-American War, and later in Panama during the building of the Canal.

*

Because Reid has so many spelling variations (Reed, Read, Ried) and because two roots are involved ('red' and 'reed') this name is notably hard to properly relate to geographic features and place names. Given the most comprehensive interpretation of the name some 6 United Kingdom towns and cities are related – Read, Reading, Reading Street, Reed, Reedham and Reedness. Canada has a Readlyn, Australia a Reedy Springs and 2 Reids, Jamaica a Reading, while the United States has 18 name-related towns and cities. Rivers, lakes, and other topographic features with variations on the name are relatively common and include Fiji's dangerous Reed Reef.

*

With about 27,000 namesakes Reid is Scotland's 11th most popular surname. Thus about one out of every 190 Scots is named Reid. (The name is not common enough throughout England and Wales to be counted separately.) Around the world Reids are most common in Canberra (one in 354 families), Vancouver (one in 563) and Toronto (one in 565). The United States has an estimated total of just under 109,000 Reids – making this their 236th most popular surname.

REILLY

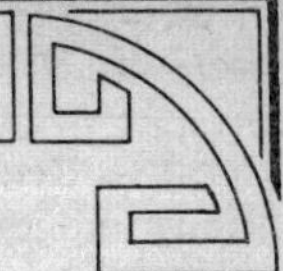

RELATED NAMES

Other surnames which are related as to root, derivation or usage include:

Orailly O'Reilly O'Riley Reily
Riley Ryley

Reilly is a widespread Irish surname which comes from the Irish Gaelic O'Raghallaigh which means 'descendant of Raghallach' ('the valiant or prosperous one'). Thus it is derived from an ancient Gaelic first name, and was probably given originally to a warrior (who would have become prosperous through booty).

The Reillys are an important family clan, which now has many subdivisions all over Ireland. However, the Reillys are still most numerous in County Cavan, where the main band of the clan is thought to have originated. The prefix 'O' is now being more frequently adopted in the anglicised form. This means 'descendant of' and is similar to the Scottish (and Irish) 'Mac-' – 'son of', and to Anglo-Norman 'Fitz-', and Welsh 'Ap-'/'Ab-', though this last does not usually appear in the original form, as more frequently it has been absorbed. The most widespread example is in the Welsh surname Bevan, which derives from Ab-Evan.

The earliest record in English sources is in the Calendar of Patent Rolls, which shows a reference to one William Orailly in 1451, though in Ireland the name certainly goes back much further than this. The anglicised forms Riley and Ryley are borrowed from a native English surname based on a common place-name type (Devon, Lancashire, etc.) meaning 'clearing where rye grows'.

A REILLY MISCELLANY

Edward O'Reilly compiled one of the first Irish-English dictionaries in 1817.

*

Hugh Reilly (1630–95) accompanied James II into exile and wrote *Ireland's Case Stated Briefly*, the only printed account of the state of Catholics in Ireland for a century.

*

Irish-born nineteenth-century newspaper editor and author Henry O'Reilly made a notable, if unusual, contribution to his adopted homeland when he contracted with inventor Samuel Morse to erect telegraph lines from Pennsylvania to the Great Lakes. He had strung over 8,000 miles of line before falling out with Morse, which event led him to abandon the project.

*

Hard-fighting US marine Lieutenant General William Riley, whose decorations included the Silver Star, the Purple Heart and the Croix de Guerre, proved to be an equally able diplomat when handed the tricky assignment of supervising United Nations military observers in potentially explosive post-war Palestine. The commission he headed tactfully settled over 1000 Arab-Israeli disputes and dealt with 65 cease-fire violations between 1948 and 1950.

*

Only one place name, Riley Hill, and no major geographic features in the United Kingdom relate to this name. It is equally rare elsewhere. The United States has 4 towns named Riley and a Rileyville and there's a Reiley Peak in Arizona.

*

In England, Scotland and Wales Reilly is not common enough to be counted separately. In Ireland with about 27,000 namesakes Reilly is the 11th most popular surname. Around the world Reillys are most common in Sydney (one in 875 families) and in Auckland (one in 1,113). In the United States there are an estimated 48,000 Reillys and 134,000 Rileys – in combination making this their 118th most popular surname.

RICHARDSON

RELATED NAMES

Other surnames which are related as to root, derivation or usage include:

Dick	Hicks	Hix	Richman
Dickens	Hickson	Reckett	Rick
Dickenson	Higgins	Ricard	Rickard
Dickson	Higginson	Rich	Rickeard
Dixon	Higgs	Richard	Rickett
Heacock	Higman	Richards	Ricketts
Hick	Hiscock	Riche	Rickman
Hickin	Hitch	Richer	Ricks
Hickman	Hitchcock	Richett	Rickson
Hickmot	Hitchison	Richey	Ritchard
Hickox	Hitchmough	Richie	Ritchie

The surname Richardson derives from one of the most popular first names in the land. The name Richard was brought to England by the Normans in 1066, and its origins are Germanic. It began life as the name Richard which, in Old German, means 'powerful – brave'.

Richard was popular right from the start and appears as a first name many times in the Domesday Book, usually Latinised to Ricardus. It was further popularised out of admiration for the valiant efforts of Richard I (known as 'The Lionheart'). Even the exploits of the next two Richards (especially the notorious hunchbacked Richard III) failed to dim its popularity.

Naturally, Richard soon began to spawn a whole number of diminutives and variations. Dick was one of the first and is still the most common – as is seen in the phrase 'every Tom, Dick and Harry'. The variation Dick gave rise to the surnames Dickens, Dickenson and Dickson.

Richard, in its standard form, gave rise to the surnames Richard, Richardson and Richards. The surname Richards – 'descendent of, dependent of, Richard' – is most common in

Cornwall, South Wales and the Midlands. Richardson, on the other hand, is common all over the country, with the exception of the West Country. The name is most popular in the north.

Other derivatives of the first name Richard (most of which have died out) gave rise to such widespread surnames as Hick, Hitch, Richie, Richey, and Rick (Ricks and Rickson), also Rich (though this is sometimes derived from a nickname), Richett (from the Old French diminutive Richot), and Rickman (which means 'servant of Richard'). Hud, sometimes a pet name for Richard, is more usually used for Hugh (see Hughes). Hitchmough and Hickmott both mean 'Richard's brother-in-law'.

The earliest mention of a form of this name as a surname is in the Hundred Rolls of 1276 for Oxford. There one Thomas Richard is mentioned.

A RICHARDSON MISCELLANY

Versatile British physicist and psychologist Lewis Fry Richardson (1881–1953) first applied mathematical techniques to predict the weather reasonably accurately. He died in Kilmun, Argyllshire, one of the wettest spots on Scotland's west coast.

*

I.A. Richards (b. 1893) English literary critic and semantics expert, was co-author of *The Meaning of Meaning*. Despite the seeming circularity of the title, it is one of the most influential books ever written on the symbolism of language.

*

Richardson's Number is the parameter used to predict the occurrence of fluid turbulence.

*

Richardson and its related names have been held by some of literature's most lasting figures. Samuel Richardson (1689–1761) is the founder of the English domestic novel. As a young man he was so proficient as a letter writer that others employed him to compose their correspondence. This led to his first successful book *Familiar Letters*, a how-to guide to letter composition. Novels, starting with *Pamela, or Virtue Rewarded*, all in epistolatory form, followed and all were vastly popular. Charles Dickens (1812–78) possibly the best-loved author of all time, drew on his impoverished childhood to write novels that exposed the hypocrisies and evils of Victorian England. All were first published in monthly instalments. The phrase 'a Dickensian childhood' has since entered the language.

*

In the United Kingdom one place name relates directly to this surname – Richards Castle. Canada has towns called Richard, Richards Landing and Richardson Station while the United States has 6 related-name towns. Geographic namesakes are common and include mountains in Canada, Australia and New Zealand, the Richards Deep in the Pacific and Richardsbreen glacier in Norway.

*

With about 104,000 namesakes Richardson is the 51st most popular surname in England and Wales. (The name is not common enough throughout Scotland to be counted separately.) Richardson is notably popular in and around Teesside where an estimated one in about 245 families bears the name. In descending numerical order Leeds, Nottingham and Bradford are other Richardson strongholds. Around the world Richards and Richardsons are most common in Canberra (one in 461 families), Wellington (one in 507) and Ottawa (one in 527). The United States tallies Richards and Richardsons together – an estimated combined total of 429,000 makes this their 34th most popular surname.

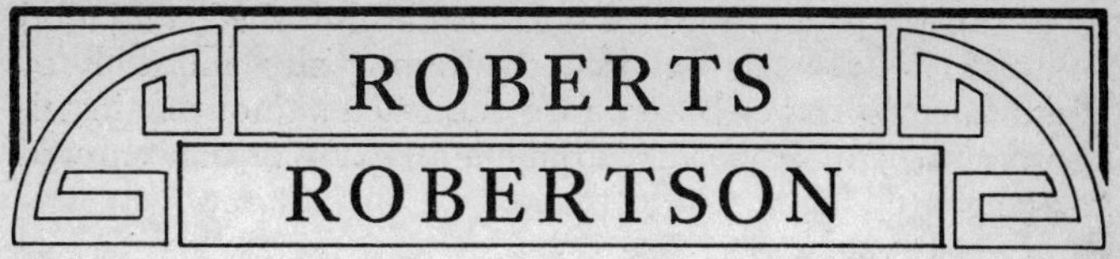

ROBERTS ROBERTSON

RELATED NAMES

Other surnames which are related as to root, derivation or usage include:

Dobbs
Dobkins
Dobson
Hobbins
Hobbs
Hobday
Hobkins
Hobson
Hopkins
Hopkinson
Nobbs
Robart
Robarts
Robb
Robbens
Robbett
Robbie
Robbins
Robers
Roberson
Robert
Robeson
Robin
Robins
Robotkin
Robson
Ropkins
see also Robinson

The surnames Roberts and Robertson come from the first name Robert.

This first name derives originally from the centuries-old German name Rodbert, which is a combination of two Old German words. These are the word 'hroth' which means 'fame' and the word 'berht' which means 'bright'. Thus the original Roberts were 'fame-bright', meaning in the literal sense much the same as our modern word 'illustrious'.

When this name spread to France it became transformed to Robert, and as such it was imported to England by the Normans in 1066. Robert soon became very popular. The first name Robert and the surname form both appear frequently in the Domesday Book. From the earliest records this name also appears in several variations, the most common being Robin which by the thirteenth century had started giving rise to variations of its own. Nowadays it is often impossible to tell which of these variations spring from the original Robert, and which from Robin. They range through Rob, Dob, Hob, Bob and Nob. In Scotland the variants, Rab, Rabbie and Robbie (as in the poet Rabbie Burns) soon appeared.

This host of variations gave rise to numerous surnames, all of which derive from the same source as Roberts and Robertson. The most common of these are Robinson (see under appropriate heading), Robbins, Robson, Robeson, Dobkins, Hobkins, and even Dobbs and Dobson. All of these mean 'son or dependant of Robert' (through a variation or diminutive). Other related names in common use include Robbett and Robb.

The earliest mention of a form of Roberts (or Robertson) used as a surname is in the Domesday Book records for Kent in 1086, where Willelmus filius Roberti is mentioned.

A ROBERTS MISCELLANY

At least two Roberts have become religious figures with a strong appeal to the common man. One was Frederick William Robertson (1816–53), also known as 'Robertson of Brighton. He was a charismatic Church of England clergyman whose eloquent and psychologically astute sermons made him widely popular among the working class. However, his ecumenical views and ideas on reform generated intense opposition from within the Church. Another is the Bible-thumping, fire-breathing US evangelist and faith healer, Oral Roberts, who draws crowds of thousands of faithful. He has founded the Oral Roberts Evangelistic Association and Oral Roberts University, both in Tulsa, Oklahoma.

*

English livery-stable owner Thomas Hobson (1554–1631) of Cambridge, earned himself a place in history with his habit of insisting customers take the horse that happened to be nearest the door. This led to the expression 'Hobson's Choice', i.e. 'this or none'.

*

Scottish choral conductor Hugh Robertson (1874–1952) founded Glasgow's noted Orpheus Choir in 1906.

*

Legendary cricketer Sir Jack Hobbs (1882–1963) was one of the greatest batsmen England ever produced. His feats include making 3,636 runs, including 12 centuries, in test matches against Australia, and a record number of 197 centuries in first-class cricket including, in 1926, the highest score at Lords (316).

*

William Dobson (1610–46) succeeded Van Dyck as portrait painter to Charles I.

*

When Sir Robert Peel founded metropolitan London's police force in 1829, constables were at first called 'Peelers', as they still are in Ireland (the term was first applied to the force Sir Robert founded in Ireland when he was Chief Secretary for that country). This was quickly superseded by the still-common term 'Bobbies', from his first name.

*

Five United Kingdom towns are related to this name: Robertson (2), Robert Hill, Robertsbridge and Roberttown. Canada has 3 Robertsvilles while the United States has 6 name-related cities and towns. Ireland has a Robertstown, Liberia a Robertsfield and a Robertsport and India a Robertsganji. Geographic namesakes are widespread.

*

With about 231,000 namesakes Roberts is the 9th most popular name in England and Wales, while with 42,000 Robertsons it is Scotland's 6th most common surname. Roberts is notably popular in and around Liverpool where an estimated one in about 125 families bears the name. In descending numerical order Cardiff, Manchester and Birmingham are other Roberts' strongholds. Robertson is notably popular in and around Edinburgh (one in 99 families bears the name). Around the world Roberts and Robertson are most common in Wellington (one in 284 families), Canberra (one in 334) and Auckland (one in 345). The United States tallies Roberts and Robertsons together – an estimated combined total of just under 550,000 making this their 19th most popular surname.

ROBINSON

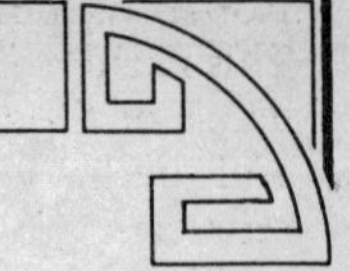

RELATED NAMES

Other names which are related as to root, derivation or usage include:

Dobbs	Hobday	Robart	Robers
Dobkins	Hobkins	Robb	Robeson
Dobson	Hobson	Robbens	Robin
Hobbins	Hopkins	Robbins	Robins
Robison	Robson	See also Robertson	

Robinson is a patronymic, in other words a name derived from the father's name. (Though inevitably, as the name was handed down, the original father became a great-grandfather and so on.) This habit of handing down names was particularly prevalent amongst the Vikings. (Even today, Ericson and Anderson feature far more prominently in the Stockholm telephone directory than Smith and Jones in the London counterpart.) For this reason it used to be assumed that all names ending in '-son' were of Viking origin – especially as many of these names originated from the north of England in the area occupied by the Vikings. Research has shown however that names ending in '-son' occurred in English before the Viking invasions, and also originated later in southern areas untouched by the Vikings.

In England, before Henry IV's reign, a son did not necessarily take on his father's name (whether by calling himself '-son' or simply by adopting the father's surname). But from this time on the practice became almost universal. (One of the last recorded instances of this *not* happening is in the 1431 records, which mention one Robertus de Lynly, filius Thomas Johnson.) In southern Lancashire, to facilitate tenure of land, daughters were occasionally named after their fathers, with the addition of '-daughter' to the original name. These awkward names quickly fell out of use, however.

Robinson (or occasionally Robison) thus derives from 'son of Robin'. Robin itself is a diminutive of the French name

Robert, popular in Normandy and England in medieval times. This French name had in turn originated from the Old German name of Rodbert, derived from 'hroth' which means 'fame' and 'berht' which means 'bright'. So the name Robert would represent a parental wish for the child's 'fame-bright' future.

After the Norman Conquest, Robert quickly became a popular name in England. It appears frequently in the Domesday Book, and has been amongst the dozen most popular first names in England ever since. The main surprise here is that England has never had a king called Robert. Scotland, on the other hand, has had several. The most famous of these was Robert the Bruce, the scourge of the English at the Battle of Bannockburn. (This may well account for the lack of Kings called Robert in England.) The naming of kings has always been a serious business, with past history and superstition often playing no small part. (No King of England would want to take on the name of his victorious Scottish counterpart.)

Despite its simplicity (or perhaps because of the popularity of those who held it) the name Robert soon spawned innumerable derivatives and nicknames. Rob, Nob and Dob were amongst the earliest – and today's more popular Bob only came on the scene several centuries later. Rab and Rob were evolved in Scotland and Northern Ireland. Robin is a diminutive of the nickname Rob, and quickly became so popular that by the middle of the thirteenth century there were more Robins than there were original Roberts. Though England may never have had a King Robert (or Robin), one of its most popular heroes is Robin Hood.

The earliest Robinson to appear in the records is one John Robynson. He is listed in the Court Rolls of the Manor of Wakefield for 1324.

A ROBINSON MISCELLANY

Londoner Henry Crabb Robinson (1775–1867) was a famous controversialist of his day, noted for giving lively Sunday morning breakfast parties that attracted literary guests like William Blake, Charles Lamb, Coleridge and the Wordsworths.

*

The modern garden owes much of its style to British landscape designer William Robinson (1838–1935). A passionate believer in the natural garden, he launched and won a vigorous lifelong campaign against the rigidly formal architectural gardens popular in his early career.

*

Noted Canadian-born US-based illustrator and political cartoonist Boardman Robinson was strongly influenced by French political cartooning in his student days. His own trenchant World War I cartoons brought him world-wide fame. He also illustrated classics like *Moby Dick* and *The Brothers Karamazov,* and created the murals in New York's Rockefeller Center and Washington DC's Department of Justice.

*

Wildly inventive illustrator W. Heath Robinson (1872–1944) specialised in drawings of incredibly complex machines which served no useful purpose. Since then any elaborate or overwrought piece of equipment has become known as a 'real Heath Robinson'.

*

There are no related geographic or place names in the United Kingdom. Both Australia and South Africa have towns called Robinson, while there are 2 such towns in the United States and in Canada. The US also has towns called Robin and Robinette, while Canada has a Robinsonville and a Robinvale. Australia has the Robinson range of mountains. The name is geographically fairly common.

*

With about 194,000 namesakes Robinson is the 14th most popular surname in England and Wales. (The name is not common enough throughout Scotland to be counted separately.) Robinson is notably popular in and around Teesside where an estimated one in about 127 families bears the name. In descending numerical order Bradford, Leeds and Sheffield are other Robinson strongholds. Around the world Robinsons are most common in Sydney (one in 502 families), Auckland (one in 515) and Wellington (one in 542). The United States has more Robinsons than the entire population of Bradford – an estimated total of just under 508,000 makes this their 22nd most popular surname.

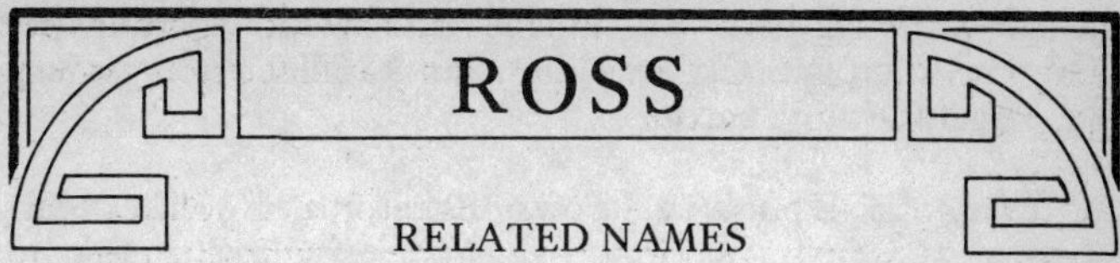

ROSS

RELATED NAMES

Other surnames which are related as to root, derivation or usage include:

Roos Rosce Rose

The surname Ross has several variations, none of which is predominant. One derivation is from the Norman French name Roce, from Old German Rozzo, which originated from personal names containing the Old German word 'hroth' – 'fame'. This word also gives us the first syllable of the name Robert (see Roberts/Robertson). So in this case Ross comes from a Norman first name of Germanic origin, and as such would have first arrived in England at the time of the Norman Conquest.

The other derivations are from a variety of place names all containing the Celtic element 'ros' or 'rhos' – 'a heath, a promontory or an isthmus'. Thus Ross would mean 'from Ross'. There are places called Ross in Herefordshire and Northumbria; there is a Scottish county of Ross. There are places called Roos in Yorkshire and Roose in Lancashire, both of which could give rise to the local surname Ross, as well. Other place names containing Ros-, Rose- and Rhos- occur in Wales, Scotland, Brittany, Ireland and Cornwall.

Another source of the name Ross is the small village of Rots in Calvados (Normandy). By this derivation the surname came across the Channel with the Normans in 1066.

The first mention of Ross as a surname appears in the Pipe Rolls of 1197 for Kent, where one Johannes filius Rosce is mentioned. The name in this instance almost certainly comes from the Norman word for fame.

A ROSS MISCELLANY

A Ross became chief of the Cherokee Indians in 1828. John Ross, also known as Kooeshoowe (1790–1866), was the son of a Scottish father and an Indian mother. For years Ross bravely resisted the encroachment of the white man and his laws on Cherokee territory, but despite all his attempts it was largely a losing battle.

*

As every US schoolboy knows, Betsy Ross (1752–1836) stitched the first American flag, at the request of George Washington. Recent historical opinion, however, has begun to doubt the authenticity of Betsy's patriotic feat.

*

The first man to discover the magnetic north pole (1831) was Sir James Clarke Ross (1800–62). This famous explorer also sailed the coasts of Antarctica, many parts of which are named after him.

*

The Nobel Prize-winning pathologist, Sir Ronald Ross (1857–1932), was a professor of tropical medicine. Best known for his investigations into malaria, he made the discovery that the disease is transmitted by the *anopheles* mosquito.

*

Fur trader and pioneer Alexander Ross left Scotland to join John Jacob Astor's 1810 expedition to the unexplored wilds of Oregon. He later helped found Astoria, Fort Walla Walla and the Red River Settlement, and left vivid accounts of his adventures in books such as *Fur Hunters of the Far West.*

*

One United Kingdom geographic feature, Rossall Point, and 9 towns and cities are related to this name, including 3 towns named Ross and Ross-on-Wye. South Africa has a Rossing while Canada has a Rossendale, Rossland, Rossport, Rossway and Rosswood. Australia and Senegal each have a Ross while Ireland has 8 Ross-related towns including Rosslare. In the United States there are 9 such towns. Geographic features named for Ross are all over the globe. There are Ross Islands in Antarctica and in Burma as well as a veritable flood of lakes and rivers and masses of mountains.

*

With about 23,000 namesakes Ross is the 15th most popular surname in Scotland. Thus one out of 230 Scots is so named. (The name is not common enough in England and Wales to be counted separately.) Around the world Ross's are most common in Vancouver (one in 712 families), Toronto (one in 809) and Auckland (one in 843). The United States has more Ross's than the entire population of Southampton – an estimated total of just over 242,000 makes this their 77th most popular surname.

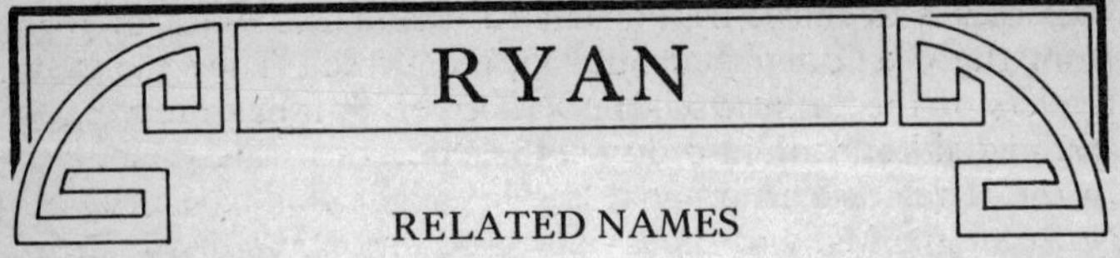

RYAN

RELATED NAMES

Other surnames which are related as to root, derivation or usage include:

Mulrine Mulryan Muroyne O'Mulrigan O'Mulryan O'Riain O'Ryan

The surname Ryan comes from the Irish O'Riaghain or O'Riain, respectively meaning 'descendant of Riaghan' and 'of Rian'. Closely related are the names O'Mulrigan (anglicised from the Irish O'Maoilriaghain) and O'Mulryan (anglicised from the Irish O'Maoilriain). These latter Irish surnames mean 'descendant of Maol-riaghain or Maol-riain'; the Maol- names mean 'follower of Riaghan' or 'of Rian'. The meaning of the name O'Maoilriaghain is disputed, but the most likely explanation is that it means 'devotee of St Iain' (Iain being the Gaelic for John), or perhaps 'Iain the Chief'.

The first name John is one of the most ancient in popular use. It derives from the Hebrew name Jochanaan (or Johanan) which means 'God is gracious'. The Crusaders introduced the Latin form Johannes into Europe, and the name quickly spread. In each country it developed its own variations, from Jan in Holland to Jean in France. In England it became John, and in Scotland it became Jock (as well as Iain). The Welsh version is Evan (giving rise to the popular surname), and the Irish version is Sean (pronounced Shawn) indicating its similarity to the French Jean.

The Ryans are one of the great Irish family clans (or septs), and the name is found all over Ireland. It is most frequent in County Tipperary, where it is four times more popular than the other two best-known names from this county (O'Brien and Mahon). Variations on the original Mulryan are still found in Galway and Leitrim in the form of Mulrine and Muroyne. O'Riain is the more usual Leinster form.

Occasionally the name Ryan derives from an entirely different source. Here the origin of the name as we know it is Ruane.

This comes from the Irish Gaelic 'O'Ruadhain', which derives from the Gaelic word 'ruadh' meaning 'red'. Thus the first holders of the name would have been given it as a nickname, alluding either to their ruddy complexion or to their red hair. In the latter case an original 'ruadh' might well have been of Norse origin. Many of the Ryans in County Mayo derive their name from the Ruane source.

A RYAN MISCELLANY

Dr James Ryan (1891–1970) was, with Eamon de Valera, a founder of the Irish political party, Fianna Fail, whose name means 'Army of Destiny'.

*

In ancient Arthurian legend and romance, Ryance, King of Wales, Ireland and The Isles, cut the beard off every knight he vanquished and made the beards into a cloak. Finding himself one short, he sent a messenger to King Arthur, demanding his beard and threatening to come and take it if necessary. Arthur refused and dispatched two knights who overcame Ryance and brought him back a prisoner.

*

Loch Ryan is an arm of the sea in southern Scotland, dividing the peninsula of Galloway from the mainland of Wigtownshire.

*

There are no name-related towns in the United Kingdom (but there is a Ryan lake) and few Ryans anywhere. The United States has 2 towns named Ryan and a Ryan Park township.

*

In England, Scotland and Wales Ryan is not common enough to be counted separately. In Ireland with about 34,000 namesakes Ryan is the 8th most popular surname. Around the world Ryans are most common in Canberra (one in 460 families), Sydney (one in 571) and Melbourne (one in 600). In the United States there are an estimated 155,000 Ryans – making this the country's 152nd most popular surname.

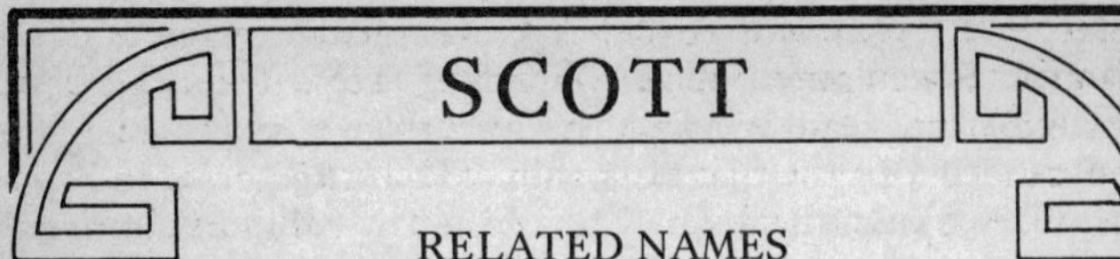

SCOTT

RELATED NAMES

Other surnames which derive from one or other of two roots include:

Scot Scotson Scotter Scotts Scutt Scutts

The surname Scott is a location or nationality name, and is the best-known example of this type of naming in the land. Naturally, one would expect the original bearers of the name to come from Scotland, and this is frequently the case – though the name has always been found most frequently in Northumbria. (A location name was most often given to someone only after he had left his place of origin – and naturally the highest concentration of people of Scottish origins would have occurred in early times just south of the border.)

However, by one of the quirks of fate, the first Scots people (long before the origin of the name) came originally from Ireland. Nowadays, the descendants of these early Hibernian immigrants are mainly found in the Highlands and the Hebrides. Most lowland Scottish people are of English origin, whereas the inhabitants of the Orkneys and the Shetlands are almost exclusively of Norse descent. This fact is not so surprising when you consider that to this day the nearest railway station to Lerwick, the main town in the Shetland Islands, is Bergen in Norway.

The surname Scott would thus originally have referred to the Gaelic origin of its holder, at least in Scotland. Just south of the border, where the name is most frequent, the name would have simply been given to someone who came from Scotland. However, the name Scott is also numerous all over England, especially in the eastern counties and in the south-west (particularly Devon). Here the original Scots may well have been settlers, or the name may have been given as a nickname – to someone considered Scottish in appearance or manner. Speculation upon the actual attributes alluded by this nickname lead one into the minefield of racialism – but one can be certain that originally the nickname would not have been sympathetic. In years gone by, rural communities tended to be insular and biased against foreigners (a trait which has not completely vanished), and for many years in previous centuries Scotland was at war with England.

The close names of Scutt and Scotter, which appear in the West Country (almost exclusively in Dorset), are usually of different origin. This is an occupational name of Old French origin, meaning 'scout' or 'spy'. However, here there are oral difficulties. Many of the original Scutts have changed through the years to Scott, and vice versa.

According to the great authority on Scottish names, Black, the surname Scott first appears in the Selkirk records which cover the years around 1124. Here one Uchtred filius Scot is mentioned.

A SCOTT MISCELLANY

Reginald Scott (1538–99) is credited with the introduction into England of hop-growing and therefore deserves a grateful nod from the nation's ale fanciers. He was also an author, although his works were not always well received: James I ordered his *The Discoverie of Witchcraft* (1584) burned.

*

The Gothic Revival triumphs of London's St Pancras Station and the Albert Memorial are the work of the architect Sir George Gilbert Scott (1811–78). Sir George's grandson, Sir Giles Gilbert Scott (1880–1960), carried on the family's architectural tradition; his contributions include Liverpool's Anglican cathedral and the new Waterloo Bridge in London.

*

Sir Peter Scott (b. 1909), ornithologist son of Captain Robert Falcon Scott, is well known for his paintings of wild fowl and illustrations for wildlife books. He was instrumental in setting up the British Wildfowl Trust at Slimbridge, and is Chairman of the World Wildlife Fund.

*

Barbara Ann Scott (b. 1928) became the first North American

to win a world championship in figure skating. That 1947 victory made her a national heroine in Canada.

*

Astronaut David R. Scott (b. 1932) commanded the Apollo 15 mission to the moon. He, James Irwin and Alfred Worden were launched on 26 July 1971, and 3½ days later landed at the base of the moon's Apennine Ridge. The team made record-breaking excursions in their lunar roving vehicle, covering 17½ miles (28 km) on three forays and racking up a combined total of 17 hours outside the module. A week after landing on the moon they were back in Houston with a huge cargo of lunar rocks (170 lb – 77 kg), having collected an unprecedented amount of valuable scientific data.

*

The combination of the nation and the explorer have led to exceptional use of this name both for places and for geographic features. Apart from the name Scotland itself, 19 UK towns contain the name. These range from Scotch Corner to Scotton. Canada has 7 name-related places, Australia a Scottsdale and South Africa a Scottburgh. The United States has 25 Scott-related places including a ghost town in Death Valley called Scotty's Castle, 3 towns called Scott and 2 Scotlands. Namesake geographic features are widespread.

*

With about 127,000 namesakes Scott is the 41st most popular surname in England and Wales. There are over 30,000 Scotts in Scotland where it is 9th in popularity. In Ireland it is estimated that with about 9,000, Scott is the 90th most popular surname. The name is notably popular in and around Edinburgh where an estimated one in about 128 families bears the name. In descending numerical order Glasgow, Teesside and Sheffield are other Scott strongholds. Around the world Scotts are most common in Vancouver (one in 425 families), Auckland (one in 464) and Wellington (one in 474). The United States has more Scotts than the entire population of Bristol – an estimated total of just over 429,000 makes this their 36th most popular surname.

SMITH

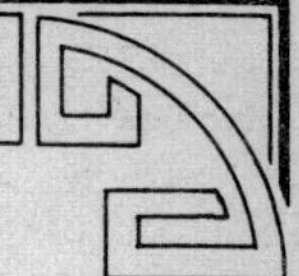

RELATED NAMES

Other surnames which are related as to root, derivation or usage include:

Arrowsmith	Haddad	Smithe	Smithson
Brownsmith	Kovac	Smither	Smithwick
Coppersmith	Lefèvre	Smitherman	Smithy
Faber	Smid	Smithers	Smyth
Goldsmith	Smisson	Smithfield	Smythe
Greensmith	Smit	Smithies	Smythman

Whitesmith

Entire books have been written about the great English name of Smith. In origin this is an occupational name and comes from the Old English word 'smith' meaning 'a metal-worker'. In this form it has remained unchanged for over 1,000 years, apart from the spelling variations of Smyth or Smythe. However, occasionally the name Smythe will in fact be a location name, deriving from Smithy. Thus it would mean 'dweller at the smithy'.

The surname Smith has also frequently become double-barrelled, as for example in Robinson-Smith. The partner name in this case would have its own entirely separate derivation; it would usually be adapted from an indirect female line. Other variations on this name derive from specific trades – such as Brownsmith (meaning 'copper or brass-smith'), or Greensmith (for 'coppersmith' – the green referring either to the patina of copper, or to the colour of the flame when it is worked), Arrowsmith and Goldsmith. London's borough of Hammersmith is named after a forge – a 'hammer-smithy'.

Besides being easily the most popular name in England, Smith is also the most popular in Scotland, and in the United States (where the name will frequently have been anglicised from foreign sources, such as the German Schmidt). In Wales, however, Smith comes second to its greatest rival, Jones.

Besides the previously mentioned German form, there are also many other foreign versions of Smith. Some of the most widespread of these are Lefèvre (the French form), Kovac (in Slavonic languages), Haddad (in Hebrew), or Faber (from the Latin). Once again, these are only the simple forms and, like our English Smith, they also have their compound forms. The lesser-known examples are the French Orfèvre (goldsmith) and the German variation Messerschmidt (knifesmith).

Early examples of the name Smith were sometimes Latinised in the records to Faber. This name appears in the records from the 1066 Domesday Book onwards. However, the surname Smith has appeared in all records from the very earliest times and pre-dates the Domesday Book. The first reference comes in the Annals for Durham in AD 975, where one Ecceard Smith is mentioned.

A SMITH MISCELLANY

One enterprising branch of the Smith family have blazoned the name on hundreds of British high streets. W.H. Smith (1792–1865) took over his father's small news-stand in 1816 and later, helped by his son – also named William Henry (1825–91), expanded the business into the largest such enterprise in Great Britain, with over 300 outlets and 20,000 employees. The younger W.H. became an MP in 1868 and served as, amongst other things, First Lord of the Admiralty (1877). He was affectionately nicknamed 'Old Morality' by *Punch* and was the butt of the famous line, 'Now I am the ruler of the Queen's Nav-ee' in Gilbert and Sullivan's 1878 operetta *HMS Pinafore.*

*

Fiery-tempered British general, Sir Harry Smith (1787–1860), was Governor of Cape Colony and High Commissioner of South Africa from 1847 to 1852. During his colourful career he took part in the Peninsular War, witnessed with horror the burning of Washington DC during the War of 1812, and fought at Waterloo. Transferred to Cape Colony during the Cape Frontier War, he made an historic ride, galloping the 600 miles from Cape Town to Grahamstown in under six days, to tell terrified colonists that help was on the way. It is his wife whose memory is recalled by the town of Ladysmith in Natal.

*

The massive Smithsonian Institution in Washington DC was founded by the bequest of over £100,000 'to the United States of America for the increase and diffusion of knowledge among men' by English scientist James Smithson (1765–1829), illegitimate son of Hugh Percy, Duke of Northumberland. He apparently made the bequest out of bitterness, writing, 'My name shall live in the memory of man when the title of the Northumberlands are extinct and forgotten.'

*

One of the best-known of all Smiths was Sydney Smith (1771–1845). Lord Macaulay called him the 'Smith of Smiths', Abraham Lincoln quoted him frequently, Charles Dickens named a son after him, and even Queen Victoria found him amusing. Clergyman, wit and essayist, Smith was lauded in his lifetime as the greatest master of trenchant ridicule since Jonathan Swift and Voltaire, although he lacked their vitriol. For a quarter of a century he deflated pomposity and exposed hypocrisy as he fought for parliamentary reform and for emancipation of Catholics. Eventually made a canon of St Paul's, he invented the still-common expression for a misfit: 'a square peg in a round hole'. This master of quotable quotes once summed up his life by saying he had spent it like a razor, 'in hot water or a scrape'.

*

The geographical centre of the United States lies in Smith County, Kansas.

*

Joseph Smith (1805–44), founder of the Mormon Church, claimed that an angel had presented him with golden plates and a book written in hieroglyphics which he translated with the aid of magic stones and had published as *The Book of the Mormon.* Having led his followers from New York State to Illinois, Smith claimed personal divinity and ruled with an iron hand until his plans to introduce polygamy caused violence and led to his arrest. While in goal he was killed by an angry mob.

*

London's major meat market, Smithfield, north of St Paul's, was long famous for its cattle sales. In the time of Mary Tudor it was the place where heretics were burnt at the stake. It takes its name from the Old English word *smethe*, meaning 'smooth'.

*

Donald Alexander Smith, Baron Strathcona and Mount Royal, served as High Commissioner for Canada from 1896 and at one time controlled both the Great Northern and the Canadian Pacific railways.

*

English-born Assyriologist George Smith (1840–76) achieved world-wide fame in 1872 by his translation of fragments of Chaldean tablets in the British Museum which described The Flood. Public interest ran so high that a London paper financed an expedition to search for the missing fragment. On the fifth day of digging Smith found it – an almost miraculous stroke of luck. His *Chaldean Account* was a nineteenth-century best-seller.

*

Smith-related places and geographic features are popular but not nearly as dominating as the surname itself. The United Kingdom has 6 towns with related names – Smith Green, Smithsfield, Smithincott, Smithston, Smithstown and Smithy Houses. Canada has a Smith, a Smithers and a Smithtown; Australia a Smithton; South Africa a Smithfield; and there's a Smith in Argentina. The United States has 26 related-name towns – all are relatively small. Related-name geographic features are common.

*

With about 837,000 namesakes Smith is the most popular surname in England and Wales. There are over 69,000 Smiths in Scotland where it is also the most popular name. In Ireland it is estimated that with about 36,000, Smith is the 5th most popular surname. Smith is notably popular in and around Leicester where an estimated one in about 55 families bears the name. In descending numerical order Nottingham, Birmingham and Coventry are other Smith strongholds. Around the world Smiths are most common in Durban (one in 109 families), Sydney (one in 110) and Auckland (one in 133).

The United States has more Smiths than the entire population of West Yorkshire – an estimated total of just over 2,501,000 makes this their most popular surname.

STEWART

RELATED NAMES

Other surnames which are related as to root, derivation or usage include:

Steuart Steward Stewardson Stewartson
Stiward Stuart

The surname Stewart (or Stuart) is a variation of the name Steward. This name is thus an occupational name, and as such it derives from the Old English word meaning 'steward or keeper of a household'. The changing of the final 'd' in the original to the more usual 't' is typical of Scottish usage, and accounts for why the name is so widespread in that country. Stewardson and Stewartson are occasional variations.

After the Norman Conquest, the rank of steward became synonymous for 'an official who controls the domestic affairs of a household' and became similar to chamberlain, though stewards were frequently more exalted in the hierarchy. For instance, the Lord High Steward of Scotland was the first officer of the Scottish kings and had the doubtful privilege of leading the Scots army into battle. Despite this hazardous occupation, a steward soon rose to the highest position in the land. Robert the Steward became King Robert II of Scotland in 1371 and founded the House of Steward (now known as the Stuarts, the French form of the word, adopted by Mary Queen of Scots).

In Scotland, steward (or stewart) was also often another name for a magistrate. For this, and the more domestic occupational reason, the name became very widespread in Scotland. Thus, only in the rarest of cases would the family name Stewart indicate royal descent (and most of these are already traced in the records).

The first mention of the surname occurs in the early records for Devon covering the years 1100–30, where one Rogere se Stiwerd appears.

A STEWART MISCELLANY

'Bonnie Prince Charlie', the Young Pretender, is one of the great heroes of Scottish history. As Charles Stuart (1720–88) he laid claim to the English throne and led the Scottish clans in the great '45 rebellion. His loyal highlanders rallied round him and he marched south, reaching as far as Derby – only to be defeated at the Battle of Culloden. After this massacre he fled to France disguised as a woman. He finally died, a drunkard, in Rome.

*

Frances Teresa Stewart (1647–1702) was the favourite of Charles II, her legendary beauty giving her the edge over her many rivals, such as Nell Gwynne. Known as 'La Belle Stewart', she was considered by Samuel Pepys as the greatest beauty of her time, and was immortalised when she posed for the image of Britannia on the coin of the realm.

*

The Australian town Alice Springs was formerly known as Stuart.

*

Scottish-born explorer John McDouall Stuart made six expeditions into the Australian interior between 1858 and 1862, finally reaching the Indian Ocean.

*

'Walking Stewart' was the baldly apt nickname bestowed upon John Stewart (d. 1822), an intrepid English wanderer who travelled on foot through Hindustan, Persia, Nubia, Abyssinia, the Arabian desert, Europe and the US.

*

The US Stuart tank, an M3 mounting a 37-millimetre gun, saw heavy action during World War II, playing a major role in the Italian Campaign and the post-D-day offensive.

*

Five towns in the United Kingdom are related – Stewartby, Stewarton (2), Stewartstown and Stuartfield. Canada has 5 as well, the United States has 9, but Australia and New Zealand have none. Both New Zealand and Chile have Stewart Islands while Australia has numerous mountains, points and bluffs named Stewart or Stuart. Name-related bodies of water and other topographic features are also common. Canada alone has 2 rivers named Stewart and 2 named Stuart.

*

There are over 41,000 Stewarts in Scotland where it is 7th in popularity. In Ireland it is estimated that with about 12,000 namesakes Stewart is the 58th most popular surname. (The name is not common enough throughout England and Wales to be counted separately.) Stewart is notably popular in and around Glasgow where an estimated one in about 140 families bears the name, while in Edinburgh the figure is one in 145. Around the world Stewarts are most common in Vancouver (one in 455 families), Wellington (one in 484) and Canberra (one in 500). The United States has more Stewarts than the entire population of Sunderland – an estimated total of just over 345,000 makes this their 47th most popular surname.

SULLIVAN

RELATED NAMES

Other surnames which are related as to root, derivation or usage include:

O'Sullivan

This popular Irish surname comes from the Gaelic O'Suileabhain meaning 'descendant of Suileabhain'. The exact meaning of the Gaelic Suileabhain is uncertain, but it is thought to mean 'black-eyed' for the first syllable is undisputably derived from the word 'suil' meaning 'an eye' – as in the similar surname O'Sullaghan which derives from the Gaelic O'Suileachain meaning 'quick-eyed'. The last part of the name may derive from some obsolete forename whose origins are now lost in the mists of time. There is speculation that it has a descriptive meaning which would compound with 'eye'. The most likely meanings of the name according to this interpretation are 'black-eyed', 'one-eyed' or 'hawk-eyed'.

Sullivan (or O'Sullivan, which means 'son of or descendant of Sullivan') is the most numerous name in Munster, and indeed the third most popular in all Ireland. The first O'Sullivans came from South Tipperary, but were driven north in the path of the Anglo-Norman invasions. They soon established themselves as the leading family clan in Munster.

This name does not appear in the early records (which are largely English and cover the mainland). The Sullivans first came to England and Scotland in appreciable numbers during the great emigrations of the nineteenth century. Here they can be found to this day in large numbers, especially in Liverpool, Glasgow, Manchester and London. However, the heaviest concentrations of O'Sullivans still crop up in Ireland. One of these is in the small seaside village of Waterville in Kerry on the far south-west coast of Ireland. Here, there are so many O'Sullivans in the village that until recently every shop and bar in the main street was called 'O'Sullivan's'.

A SULLIVAN MISCELLANY

To this day, the most popular of all light operas remain those written by Gilbert and Sullivan, *The Mikado*, *HMS Pinafore* and *Trial by Jury* being their most-performed works. Sir Arthur Seymour Sullivan (1842–1900) was the musical half of the partnership and also composed several successful symphonies and concertos in his youth. He also wrote that epitome of Victorian parlour songs, 'The Lost Chord'.

*

Perhaps the greatest of all American prize-fighters was the celebrated John L. Sullivan (1858–1918). 'The Great John L.' could not only knock out all comers with his fists, he could also drink all comers under the table. He earned over $1 million in his career, and his flamboyant personality contributed to his legendary status. Ironically, later in life, reformed by his second wife, he ended up lecturing on the temperance circuit.

*

Cartoon character Felix the Cat was the creation of the Australian newspaper cartoonist, Pat Sullivan (1887–1933), who emigrated to the US.

*

Places and geographic features incorporating the name Sullivan are relatively rare. Only the United States has towns which are so named – 5 called Sullivan and one Sullivanville. Canada has a Sullivan lake as well as 2 named O'Sullivan, also a Sullivan Bay. Off the coast of Burma there is a Sullivan Island.

*

In England, Scotland and Wales Sullivan is not common enough to be counted separately. In Ireland with about 46,000 namesakes Sullivan is the 3rd most popular surname. Around the world Sullivans are most common in Auckland (one in 556 families), Canberra (one in 742) and Sydney (one in 836). In the United States there are an estimated 241,000 Sullivans – making this the country's 79th most popular surname.

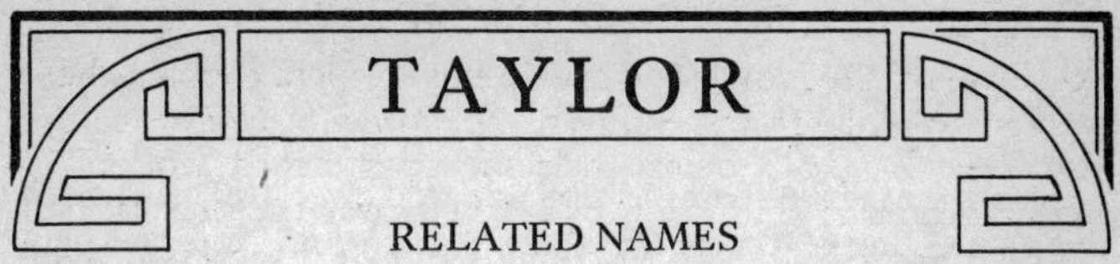

TAYLOR

RELATED NAMES

Other surnames which are related as to root, derivation or usage include:

Tailer Taille Tailor Tayler
Taylerson Taylorson Taylour

The surname Taylor is an occupational name from the trade we today spell as tailor. The name derives from the Middle English word 'tayler' or 'tailor'. Through the centuries the convention has gradually been established that the surname is spelt with a 'y' and the name for the trade is spelt with an 'i' – though this is not invariably the case. The Middle English word comes originally from the Old French word 'tailleur', meaning 'cutter'. This Old French source has given rise to several types of 'cutter'. The best-known one has given us the surname Talboys, which has nothing to do with youth or height. This comes from the Old French 'taillebois', which means 'cutter of wood'.

The surname Taylor is thus of Norman origin and came to England with William the Conqueror. Incidentally, it also gave the lie to the exclusiveness of Norman names. Taylor does not sound as Norman as, say, the more numerically exclusive de la Tour, but it is just as old and just as French.

There are several well-known variations on the most usual spelling – Taylor. They range through Tailer, Tayler or Taylour to Taylorson and Taylerson.

References to the surname Taylor start appearing in the records from the twelfth century on. One of the earliest of these is in the Pipe Rolls for Somerset. In the records for the year 1182 one William le Taillur appears. Here the Norman origin and the occupational derivation are well illustrated.

A TAYLOR MISCELLANY

Donald P. Taylor of Sage, California, circumnavigated the globe in the smallest aircraft so far. He built the plane in his garage, all 20 ft 11 in (6.38 m) of it. The single 180 hp Thorp T-18 engine completed the journey in 37 stages, taking a total of 176 flying hours.

*

Scottish dramatist Tom Taylor adapted over 100 works for the stage. One of them, *Our American Cousin,* was the play Abraham Lincoln was watching when he was assassinated.

*

In 1948 Sir William Francis Kyffin Taylor became, at 93, the oldest person ever raised to the peerage.

*

Thespian Joseph Taylor was an Englishman mentioned in Shakespeare's *First Folio* as one of the 26 actors who took principal parts in all those plays. Legend has it that the Bard himself coached Taylor in the role of Hamlet.

*

The Taylor Standard Series is the method used to discover which characteristics of a ship's hull govern its water resistance. Its inventor, David Watson Taylor, became a rear admiral in the US Navy and designed the first plane to fly the Atlantic (1919).

*

Coventry-born Edward Taylor (d. 1729) is considered to be colonial America's finest poet but, at his request, the best of his verse was not published until over 200 years after his death.

*

British mathematician Brook Taylor (1685–1731) is noted for his great contributions to the development of calculus – he postulated 'Taylor's Theorem'.

*

John Henry Taylor (1871–1963) was one of 'the great triumvirate' (with Harry Vardon and James Braid) which won the British Open (golf) Championship 16 times between 1894 and 1914 (Taylor won five times). Later he was a founder and the first chairman of the British Professional Golfers' Association.

*

A.J.P. Taylor (b. 1906), prolific English historian, wrote the celebrated study *Origins of the Second World War* which is considered the definitive work on the subject.

*

There are no Taylor-related places or major geographic features in the United Kingdom. Canada has a town called Taylor. The United States has 10 such towns as well as 5 Taylorsvilles, a Taylors, a Taylor Bridge and a Taylor Springs. South Africa boasts a town called Tayler's Pan while New Zealand has one delightfully named Taylor's Mistake. Virtually all of the foregoing, except the UK, have other geographic features named Taylor.

*

With about 371,000 namesakes Taylor is the 5th most popular surname in England and Wales. There are over 25,000 Taylors in Scotland where it is 14th in popularity. Taylor is notably popular in and around Manchester where an estimated one in about 115 families bears the name. In descending numerical order Birmingham, Bradford and Leeds are other Taylor strongholds. Around the world Taylors are most common in Wellington (one in 249 families), Auckland (one in 270) and Sydney (one in 305). The United States has more Taylors than the entire populations of Liverpool and Portsmouth combined – an estimated total of just under 731,000 makes this their 12th most popular surname.

THOMAS THOMPSON

RELATED NAMES

Other surnames which are related as to root, derivation or usage include:

MacThomas	Thomlinson	Tomalin	Tomkin
Thomason	Thompkin	Toman	Tomkins
Thomasson	Thompkins	Tomas	Tomkinson
Thomaston	Thompsett	Tombleson	Tomlin
Thomazin	Thompstone	Tomblin	Tomlinson
Thomerson	Thoms	Tombling	Tompkin
Thomkins	Thomsen	Tombs	Tompkins
Thomkinson	Thomson	Tomison	Tompsett
	Tomsett	Tomson	

The surnames Thomas and Thompson both derive from the first name Thomas. The first name is one of the most ancient still in popular use, deriving from the ancient Aramaic where it meant 'twin'. Its popularity in Western Europe stems from the Apostle of the same name, though in fact his real first name was Judas, and Thomas was only his nickname (given to distinguish him from Judas Iscariot).

In early days Thomas was not one of the great popular names, largely because of its link with 'Doubting Thomas' – an unwise connotation in times when heretics were drawn and quartered. However, the fortunes of this name revived in England after 1170, when Thomas à Becket (who was later canonised) was murdered in Canterbury Cathedral at the instigation of his erstwhile friend, King Henry II. In fact, there are two other English St Thomas's – St Thomas of Hereford, and Sir Thomas More (the hero of *A Man for all Seasons*) who was executed by King Henry VIII for refusing to admit the King as head of the Church.

The first name Thomas soon became the most popular in the land – witness its use in the phrase 'every Tom, Dick and Harry'. It also became synonymous for anything male (thus we get the words Tomcat and Tomboy) and to this day it is the popular name for an English soldier (Tommie).

The first name Thomas, besides giving rise to the identical surname, also gave rise to many derivations from nicknames and variations. Thus we get Tomkin, which gave rise to Tomkins and Tomkinson. It is easy to see (in terms of English pronunciation) how the middle 'p' crept into these variant surnames – as in Thompkins. This also accounts for the 'p' in Thompson. Scottish pronunciation did not find a need for the intrusive 'p' and consequently we find the spelling Thomson chiefly in Scotland.

The first name Thomas appears frequently in the Domesday Book, but it is nearly 200 years before we find the first use of the name as a surname. This is in the Hundred Rolls for Wiltshire in 1275, where one Walter Thomas is mentioned. Early in the next century the first Thompsons start appearing in the records. The first mention of the Scottish variation is in the records for Carrick in 1318, where one John Thomson is listed.

A THOMAS MISCELLANY

Scottish engineer Robert William Thomson was well ahead of his time. In 1845 he patented the pneumatic tyre, but nearly 50 years passed before Dunlop revived his invention for use in bicycles.

*

Newspaper magnate Roy Thomson (1894–1978), first Baron of Fleet, was the Canadian-born owner of the world's largest publishing empire. In 1953 he moved to the UK and successively bought *The Scotsman*, *The Sunday Times* and *The Times* itself.

*

Scottish biologist Sir Charles Wyville Thomson (1830–82) led the famous *Challenger* expedition, the first important attempt at deep-sea exploration (1872–76). He discovered many life forms previously believed extinct, sometimes as far down as 650 fathoms.

*

The deadly Thompson sub-machine gun (popularly known as

the 'Tommy Gun') was the co-invention of American Army engineer John Taliaferro Thompson (1860–1940).

*

Sir Benjamin Thompson (1753–1814), later Count Rumford, was a physicist, administrator and founder of the Royal Institution of Great Britain. His contributions to society include the cultivation of the potato, the invention of the kitchen range and a drip coffee pot, and the exposition of 'Count Rumford's Principle' concerning the cure of smoking chimneys.

*

M. Thomson was one of over fifty pseudonyms used by the French writer and philosopher, François Marie Arouet, better known as Voltaire.

*

The youngest recorded university entrant was William Thomson, later Lord Kelvin, who entered Glasgow University in October 1834, aged 10 years, 4 months.

*

The English geologist Herbert Henry Thomas (1876–1935) established that the bluestones at Stonehenge had been transported 200 miles from the Prescelly Mountains in Wales where they had been quarried.

*

Physicist Sir Joseph John Thomson (1856–1940) established in 1897 that cathode rays were moving particles, later called electrons. This led to the discovery of isotopes and a greater understanding of atomic structure.

*

The world is full of Thomas/Thomson/Thompson-related places and geographic features. The United Kingdom alone has 21 towns ranging from Tomatin to Thomshill. Canada has 5 towns, the United States 28, Australia 3 and South Africa 2. Other places are spread all over the earth from Tomas Barron in Bolivia to Thomson Village in Singapore. Name-related lakes, rivers, mountains and islands are also common.

*

With about 245,000 namesakes Thomas is the 8th most popular surname in England and Wales, while with 190,000 Thompson ranks as 15th. (Thomas is not common enough throughout Scotland to be counted separately.) Thomson has about 42,000 namesakes which makes it Scotland's 5th most popular surname. Thomas is notably popular in and around Cardiff where an estimated one in about 45 families bears the name, while Thompson's most popular area is Teesside where one in 140 families is so named. Around the world Thomas's and Thompsons (with or without the middle 'p') are most common in Wellington (one in 191 families), while Melbourne and Sydney tie for second place with one in 210. The United States has an estimated total of just under 722,000 Thomas's which makes this their 11th most popular surname, and just over 667,000 Thompsons which makes this their 16th most popular surname. Combined, they are in 6th place.

TURNER

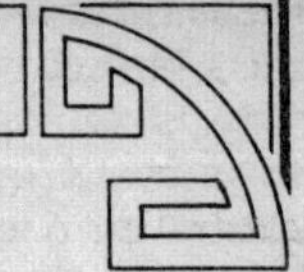

RELATED NAMES

Other surnames which are related as to root, derivation or usage include:

Tourneour Turnehare Turnor Turnour
Turnpenny Turnur

Turner has several derivations, dating from antiquity to comparatively recent times. All of these derivations are occupational – in other words, stemming from some form of work or activity. In earlier times, when society was less complex, a man *was* what he did. Common examples of this are the names Archer, Shepherd, Hornblower and Goldsmith.

The earliest derivation of Turner (or Turnour, or Turnor) is from the Old French word 'tournour'. This means 'one who turns or fashions objects of wood, metal, bone, etc. on a lathe'. The reason there are so many Turners today is because in medieval times there was a great variety of objects which could be 'turned'. Most frequently these were measures for wine and ale, or round pieces of wood for chairlegs. The lathes used by these turners bore little relation to the one you'll find in a modern workshop, though the principle was the same. The ancient lathe almost certainly evolved originally from the potter's wheel – although it's thought unlikely that the names Turner and Potter were ever synonymous. In medieval times there was little call for rounded chairlegs, except amongst the gentry at The Hall.

The turners were a sub-branch of the trade of cabinetmakers, which included many carpentering skills whose practitioners took on the name of their skill. Hence the Turners were closely related (by trade at least) to the Carvers, Dishers (fashioners of wooden dishes) and Arkwrights (chest makers).

A secondary derivation of Turner is from the Old French word 'tournoieur' which meant 'one who takes part in a tourney or tournament'. However, it's likely that only very few modern Turners derive their name from this fine medieval pastime.

The last but probably the most intriguing derivation of the name Turner comes from the old word 'turnehare'. In medieval times this was the man who ran after the hare and he literally 'turned' it into the path of the waiting hunters. Needless to say, these Turners (or Turnehares) had to be fast runners, and soon the name became synonymous with what we would term a sprinter. The name may also have had derogatory connotations. A Turnehare (the opposite of a Turnbull) was someone who only had sufficient courage to turn a hare (or perhaps run away like a hare). Turnpenny was a nickname for a miser.

The earliest Turner in the records is one Warner le Turnur, who appears in the 1180 Pipe Rolls for London.

A TURNER MISCELLANY

The Worshipful Company of Turners, founded in England in 1604, is still a thriving guild of makers of lathe-turned wooden articles.

*

English soldier Sir Tomkyns Hilgrove Turner (1766–1843) brought the Rosetta Stone back from North Africa's Alexandria. Dating from the time of Ptolemy V (*c.* 195 BC), it is covered in inscriptions in Ancient Greek and both demotic and hieroglyphic Egyptian. His ability to decipher it unlocked the secrets of other inscriptions and led to an intensive study of Egyptian antiquity. The stone is now displayed in the British Museum.

*

Sixteenth-century botanist William Turner (1520–68) introduced scientific botany into England. The many plants he named include hawkweed and goatsbeard.

*

Joseph Mallord Turner (1775–1851) is generally acknowledged to be one of England's greatest landscape painters. His impressionistic use of light and colour is world-famous. Celebrated and wealthy in his time, he died a virtual recluse leaving over 20,000 watercolours and 300 paintings to the nation.

*

One town in the United Kingdom is a namesake – Turner's Hill. Australia has a town named Turner while the United States has 6 towns so named as well as a Turners Falls, Turnercrest, Turnersville and Turnerville. Given the popularity of the surname remarkably few geographic features are Turners. Australia does have a mountain and a river which are so named.

*

With about 167,000 namesakes Turner is the 23rd most popular surname in England and Wales. (The name is not common enough throughout Scotland to be counted separately.) Turner is notably popular in and around Sheffield where an estimated one in about 255 families bears the name. In descending numerical order Bradford, Birmingham and Nottingham are other Turner strongholds. Around the world Turners are most common in Wellington (one in 607 families), Canberra (one in 639) and Auckland (one in 678). The United States has more Turners than the entire population of Coventry – an estimated total of just under 346,000 makes this their 46th most popular surname.

WALKER

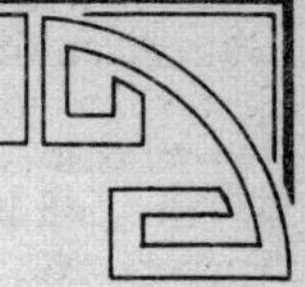

RELATED NAMES

Other surnames which are related as to root, derivation or meaning include:

Fuller Tucker Walkare Walkere

The surname Walker comes from the Old English 'wealcere', which is another name for a fuller. A fuller or walker was a person who trod cloth in a trough in the fulling process, which is mentioned in the fourteenth-century poem *Piers Plowman* where it is said:

Cloth that cometh fro the wevying (i.e. weaving)
Is nought comely to were
Tyl it be fulled under fote.

Thus the stamping and pressing practised by the walker or fuller required much the same attributes as a modern-day grape presser in Spain or France.

The name Walker is popular all over England, but is found in greatest concentration along a band stretching up from Nottingham and Derby through West Yorkshire to Durham. However, in the Durham region and in Northumbria the name Walker may occasionally be a place name, originally being given to a person who came from Walker in Northumbria. This name is a derivation of 'marsh by the (Roman) wall'. This derivation comes out more clearly in the close name Waller, which in one variation comes from being a location name for 'a dweller at the wall'.

The surnames Fuller and Tucker derive from the same profession.

The first mention of the surname Walker is in the Documents for the Abbey of Bec, where in the 1248 records for Warwickshire one Richard le Walkere is mentioned.

A WALKER MISCELLANY

The Walker Cup is a golf trophy awarded to the winner of a competition between amateur men's teams from the United

States and the British Isles. Held every other year since 1922, the venue alternates between the two countries.

*

One of the earliest American feminists was Mary Edwards Walker (1832–1919). She attracted attention to the cause by wearing men's clothes, and later served as a nurse during the American Civil War. In 1897 she established a women's colony known as 'Adamless Eden'.

*

There are 8 towns in the United Kingdom which are name related – Walker, Walker Fold, Walkerburn, Walkeringham, Walkerith, Walkering, Walker's Green and Walkerton. Canada also has a Walkerton, while the United States has 13 Walker-related towns including 7 Walkers. Both South Africa and Australia have Walkervilles. Walker-named geographic features are common and include Walker Coy Island in the Bahamas.

*

With about 180,000 namesakes Walker is the 18th most popular surname in England and Wales. There are over 19,000 Walkers in Scotland where the name is 26th in popularity. Walker is notably popular in and around Leeds where an estimated one in about 145 families bears the name. In order Teesside, Bradford and Nottingham are other Walker strongholds. Around the world Walkers are most common in Auckland (one in 449 families), Wellington (one in 460) and Canberra (one in 479). The United States has more Walkers than the entire population of Manchester – an estimated total of just over 510,000 makes this their 21st most popular surname.

WALSH

RELATED NAMES

Other surnames which are related as to root, derivation or meaning include:

Brannagh	Wallace	Walshman	Welchman
Brannick	Wallis	Walsingham	Wellis
Walch	Wallus	Walsman	Wellish
Waleys	Walshe	Welch	Wellsman
Welsh		Welshman	

The surname Walsh is a location name, more recognisable in the rarer form Welsh. Walsh derives from the Old English words 'walh', 'wealh' and 'welise', all of which mean 'a man from Wales'. However, the original meaning was much wider than our geographical interpretation and covered anyone who was a Briton, Celt, Welshman, or even just a foreigner. Much as once the word Gaul had more than French Gallic connotations – the French still call Wales Pays de Galles, and the native language of Scotland and Ireland is Gaelic.

The name Walsh is now mainly of Irish origin, and in Gaelic is written Breatnach (which means Welshman). This Gaelic name has sometimes been re-anglicised as Brannagh or Brannick – so anyone with these names is, in a way, a Walsh. However, the Irish Walshes have no family clan and are scattered all over the country. Theirs is easily the most numerous name which has no sept (or family clan), being the fourth most popular last name – and this suggests that they may originally have been foreigners, probably of Briton origin.

The surname Walsh has a large number of variations. The most widespread of these are Welch (found chiefly in East Anglia and the West Country), Welshman, Walch and Welchman. Wallace and Wallis are almost certainly the Scottish versions of this name. Though here again a Wallace would probably have been a man of Briton origin, rather than what we would call Welsh.

The surname Walsh has long been widespread in the country, and appears in many early records. The earliest reference to this name yet noted is in the 1273 Wiltshire Assize Rolls where one Henry le Waleis is listed.

A WALSH MISCELLANY

To 'welsh' on a deal means to fail to keep a promise to fulfil an obligation, notably a bet. The saying first arose in Ireland where emigrating Welshmen kept to themselves and were not trusted.

*

Welsh rarebit has been a favoured British dish for over 200 years.

*

Nicholas Welsh (d. 1585) as the Irish Bishop of Ossory had the Protestant service printed in Gaelic, which dramatically increased the number of converts. He was stabbed to death by a parishioner he had condemned for adultery.

*

Henry le Walleis served a remarkable three terms as Lord Mayor of London (1273, 1281–1283, 1298), while Sir Cullum Welch was Mayor in 1966.

*

The first pure still life – a partridge, gauntlets and arrows pinned against a wall – was painted in 1504 by Jacobo de Barbari. When this Venetian painter moved to Germany, as a guest and adviser to Dürer, he took on the name Walch.

*

The United Kingdom has 3 Walsh-related place names, the picturesquely named Walsham Le Willows, Walsham and Walshfort. Canada has 2 towns called Walsh while the United States has but one and no other towns which are related. Curiously few major geographic features are namesakes. Walsh river and Walsh mountain in Canada are exceptions.

*

In England, Scotland and Wales Walsh is not common enough to be counted separately. In Ireland with about 44,000 namesakes Walsh is the 4th most popular surname. Around the world Walsh's are most common in Sydney (one in 904 families), Canberra (one in 1,045) and Melbourne (one in

1,101). In the United States there are an estimated 119,000 Walsh's – making this the country's 214th most popular surname.

WARD

RELATED NAMES

Other surnames which are related as to root, derivation or meaning include:

Hayward	Warden	Wardrobe	Waredraper
McWard	Warder	Wardrop	Watcher
Millward	Wardes	Wardropper	Watchman
Warde	Wardman	Wardrupp	Weard
	Whatrup	Woodward	

Ward stems directly from the Old English word 'weard', which means 'one who watches or guards something'. This could be a relatively lowly social position, as in the name de Wardrobe (a variety of chamberlain or room-servant), or a position of comparative power, such as the ward of a castle or an entire estate. In this case the position could often last for many years when, for example, the Lord Mayor of London went off on a Crusade; then the official would be a nobleman in all but name.

To this day the word ward still retains its ancient meaning of guard, guardian or watchman. Someone (usually a minor) who is considered to be in need of protection can still be made a 'ward of court'.

When names described a characteristic or the occupation of the holder, they frequently retained the French 'le' (or sometimes 'la') which was inserted between the Christian name and the surname. Thus we find the names Robert le Rouge (Robert the red in face, or red-haired) and William le Ward. Nowadays the French article has almost entirely vanished, but in earlier times it would often come and go almost at whim. In the records for 1317 we come across one Robert Ward, who was also known on occasion as Robert le Ward, Robert la Ward, and even Robert de la Ward. A wardroper looked after the King's wardrobe, i.e. his stock of robes, ceremonial apparel etc.

There are many variations on the original Ward, denoting

particular occupations. Thus Woodward was originally somebody who guarded a wood, Millward guarded a mill, and Hayward guarded enclosed fields from straying cattle. Other guardians which come into the same category as the Wards are Bridgeman (often in the Frenchified form of Ponter), plain Guard (or Garth), Watchman, Wakeman, or Yeoman.

The name Ward is often found in Scotland and Ireland, somtimes in the form McWard. Here the derivation is different from the English version. The root word in this case is the Gaelic 'bhard', which means 'bard, poet or minstrel'. So the Gaelic original would have been a travelling songster.

From earliest times the name Ward was both frequent and widespread. One John Warde is mentioned in the Pipe Rolls for Yorkshire in 1194, while in the Hundred Rolls for 1273 there is a William le Warde in Oxford, a Simon le Ward in Buckinghamshire, and two further le Wardes, one in Hampshire and one in Cambridgeshire.

A WARD MISCELLANY

The creator of one of fiction's most endearing popular villains, the sinister Chinese criminal genius Dr Fu Manchu, was British-born writer Arthur Sarsfield Ward (1883–1959) who wrote under the pseudonym Sax Rohmer.

*

Winston Churchill's wartime codename was Colonel Warden. This probably stemmed from the fact that he had been made a Warden of the Cinque Ports.

*

Pioneering British philosopher/psychologist James Ward (1843–1925) has been labelled the first functional psychologist because of his emphasis on activity of the self. His celebrated article 'Psychology' (1886) appeared in the 9th edition of the *Encyclopaedia Britannica.*

*

Vanity Fair caricaturist Leslie Ward, using the pseudonym 'Spy', skewered many a notable with his acid-tipped pen in a 40-year career beginning in 1873. Reproductions of his prints sold in the thousands. In 1918 the Establishment honoured this brilliant iconoclast with a knighthood.

*

Ward-related places and geographic features are common. In the United Kingdom alone 12 towns ranging from Ward Green to Wardy Mill are namesakes. Canada has 3 such towns as does the United States, while South Africa has one named Warden. New Zealand has a town named Ward as well as a Ward mountain and a Ward Island. Bodies of water named for Ward are rare. Canada has a Ward river and South Africa a Warden's Vlei lake.

*

With about 135,000 namesakes Ward is the 36th most popular surname in England and Wales. (The name is not common enough throughout Scotland to be counted separately.) Ward is notably popular in and around Sheffield where an estimated one in about 240 families bears the name. In descending numerical order Leicester, Leeds and Nottingham are other Ward strongholds. Around the world Wards are most common in Sydney (one in 720 families), Wellington (one in 843) and Brisbane (one in 973). The United States has more Wards than the entire population of Plymouth – an estimated total of just under 270,000 makes this their 63rd most popular surname.

WATSON

RELATED NAMES

Other surnames which are related as to root, derivation or usage include:

Gaulter	Walters	Watkin	Watt
Gaultier	Waterman	Watkins	Watters
Gautier	Waters	Watkinson	Watterson
Walter	Waterson	Watmough	Wattes
	Watts	Wattson	

The surname Watson literally means 'son of Wat'. The first name Wat is a diminutive of the first name Walter (as in Wat Tyler, the leader of the Peasants' Revolt during the reign of Richard II). This derivation arose because in medieval times the usual pronunciation of Walter was Water.

The first name Walter derives from the Old German name Waldhari. This is made up of two words – 'wald' meaning 'rule', and 'hari' meaning 'army'. So some original Walters may have been war leaders.

The first name Walter came to England with the Norman Conquest and appears frequently as a first name in the Domesday Book (where it was invariably Latinised to Walterius). Right through to the mid-seventeenth century it was more customary to pronounce this first name Water, and in consequence the popular diminutive Wat (or Watt) gave rise to that surname.

Other variations of names from the first-name source of Walter include Watts (short for Watson) and Watmough ('Walter's brother-in-law'). Waters (short for Walter's son, derived from the early pronunciation of the surname as Waters) is also a derivation from a place name for a 'dweller by the water or stream'.

The surname Watson is widespread throughout the land, but appears most numerously in the north of England and the southern Scottish counties.

The earliest appearance of the name Watson in the records

is in the 1324 Rolls for the Manor of Wakefield in Yorkshire, when one Richard Watson is listed.

A WATSON MISCELLANY

Watsons and Watts have excelled in many fields of science. The Scottish inventor James Watt (1736–1819) is generally credited with the invention of the steam engine, for which he was granted a patent in 1769; the watt, a unit of power, is named after him and he also coined the term 'horsepower'; another of his inventions was the duplicating machine, to make quick copies of his records. Another Scotsman, the physicist Sir Robert Alexander Watson-Watt (1892–1973) was knighted in 1942 for his role in the development of radar (Radio Detection And Ranging), a device for locating aircraft which played a vital part in the defence of Britain against German bombing raids in World War II. Another, Dr Thomas A. Watson, worked as assistant to Alexander Graham Bell when he made the first trans-Atlantic telephone call in 1915. The American geneticist, James D. Watson (b. 1928), won a Nobel Prize in 1962 for his crucial role in the discovery of the molecular structure of DNA, the vital constituent in the genetic process.

*

In August 1965 Watts Riot in the Los Angeles ghetto (35,000 inhabitants) was the first big race riot in American history. Five days of burning, shooting and looting left 34 dead, 200 buildings destroyed and led to 3,900 arrests.

*

Charles Watson-Wentworth, Marquis of Rockingham (1730–82), made a large bet that he could drive a coach and horses at full gallop through the eye of a needle. He then craftily built a 40-foot obelisk with a large opening at the base and won the wager. The 'Needle's Eye Folly' still stands at Wentworth in Yorkshire as a memorial to his ingenuity.

*

English clergyman Isaac Watts (1674–1748) wrote hundreds of hymns, including 'O God Our Help in Ages Past' and 'When I Survey the Wondrous Cross'.

*

British-born chemist Richard Watson (1737–1816) was

credited with saving the government £100,000 in 1787 with his improvements to gunpowder.

*

Places and geographic features named for Watson are rare. There are none in the United Kingdom, one each in Canada and Australia (towns called Watson), while the United States has 3 towns so named along with a Watsonton and a Watsonville. No major mountains are so named and only a few bodies of water: Canada's Watson lake and Watson river and Australia's Watson bay.

*

With about 118,000 namesakes Watson is the 43rd most popular surname in England and Wales. There are over 21,000 Watsons in Scotland where it is 17th in popularity. Watson is notably popular in and around Edinburgh where an estimated one in about 195 families bears the name. In descending numerical order Teesside, Glasgow and Leeds are other Watson strongholds. Around the world Watsons are most common in Wellington (one in 562 families), Canberra (one in 605) and Auckland (one in 607). The United States has more Watsons than the entire population of Derby – an estimated total of just over 252,000 makes this their 71st most popular surname.

WHITE

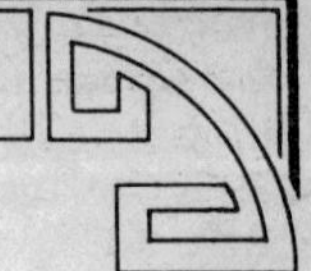

RELATED NAMES

Other surnames which are related as to root, derivation or meaning include:

Whitaker	Whitelock	Whitmarsh	Whittick
Whitbread	Whiteman	Whitmee	Whittin
Whitebread	Whiter	Whitmill	Whitting
Whitecross	Whiterod	Whitmore	Whittingham
Whitefield	Whiteside	Whitnall	Whittington
Whiteford	Whitesmith	Whitnell	Whittle
Whitehair	Whiteson	Whitney	Whittlesey
Whitehall	Whitewax	Whitson	Whittlock
Whitehead	Whitewood	Whitt	Whittome
Whitehill	Whitfield	Whittaker	Whitton
Whitehorn	Whitford	Whittall	Whitty
Whitehouse	Whitham	Whittam	Whitwell
Whiteing	Whiting	Whittard	Whitworth
Whiteland	Whitley	Whittemore	Whyte
Whitelaw	Whitlock	Whitten	Wight
Whiteley	Whitman	Whitter	Witte
	Witten	Witts	

The surname White derives from the Old English word 'Hwit' meaning the colour white. This name would thus have originated as a nickname, given say, to someone who had a white or fair complexion or hair, and it came to be a Christian name too.

Another, rarer, derivation is from the name Wight. This also is a nickname, but from the Old Norse, and means 'valiant, strong, nimble'. It is possible, but unlikely, that some instances of Wight may have been taken from the place-name form, for someone who came from the Isle of Wight.

Another, very rare, derivation of the surname White is as a place name for someone who came from the village of White. There are two such villages. One is in Huntingdonshire (where the name derives from the Old English for 'a bend in the river'), and the other is in Devon (where the name derives from the Old French for 'a look-out place').

There are innumerable variations of the original name White. The most widespread of these are Whyte, Witt (which as Witte is the Dutch form) and Witts. These gave rise to Whiteson, Whitesmith (an occupational name for a tinsmith, tin being traditionally white), Whiter (an occupational name from the Old English for a whitewasher). And there are numerous surnames such as Whitehall, Whitelaw, etc., which are derived from place names and objects containing White-. Whitebread, however, is a nickname – 'white beard'.

The name White was well established in this country long before the Norman Conquest, and even rose in popularity when the Normans arrived. The first reference to the surname White appears in the pre-Conquest annals for Herefordshire, where one Purcil Hwita was listed in 1038.

A WHITE MISCELLANY

The Bank of England, in Threadneedle Street, is haunted by a ghost known as the Black Nun, who wanders dismally about the Bank garden, formerly an old churchyard. She is said to be Sarah Whitehead, whose brother Philip was a Bank employee arrested for forging cheques in 1811 and condemned to death. Sarah went mad with grief and for the next 25 years journeyed daily to the Bank looking for her brother. She was buried in the adjacent churchyard, and has reputedly been sighted many times since.

*

America's highest peak, Mount Whitney in Southern California, is named in honour of geologist Josiah Whitney.

*

Lord Mayors of London have included many Whites: Richard Whytyngdone (1397, 1406, 1419), William White (1489), Thomas Whyte (1553), John Whyte (1563), Sir Thomas White (1876) and James Whitehead (1888).

*

Whitworth Standard screw threads are named after Sir Joseph Whitworth, the British mechanical engineer of tool-making fame.

*

The White House, official residence of US Presidents at 1600 Pennsylvania Avenue, acquired its name when a coat of white paint was hurridly slapped on to cover scorch marks incurred during the War of 1812, when the British stormed Washington.

*

White's, the noted gentlemen's club in St James's, London, was established in 1693 as a chocolate-house, and named after its proprietor.

*

As a colour-related surname White has remarkable representation both in terms of place names and geographic features all over the world. No fewer than 77 United Kingdom towns and cities are namesakes. These range from Whiteabbey to Whitewreath and include the colourfully named Whitechurch Canonicorum. Great Britain also has rivers called the Whiteadder Water and the White Esk, and a White Coomb mountain. Canada has 13 name-related towns. The United States has 78, which range from White Bird to Whitewright and include a number that reflect on life in the midst of the Indians, such as Whiteface and White Settlement. Australia has a White Mark and a White Well, New Zealand a White Rock hill, while South Africa has towns called Whites and Whitesands. There are many White mountains, being so named for the presence of year-round snow. White and White Water rivers are often so called because they run swiftly and create white water.

*

With about 204,000 namesakes White is the 12th most popular surname in England and Wales. There are over 10,000 Whites in Scotland where it is 71st in popularity. In Ireland it is estimated that with about 14,000, White is the 12th most popular surname. White is notably popular in and around Bristol where an estimated one in about 240 families bears the name. Around the world Whites are most common in Canberra (one in 377 families), Sydney (one in 414) and Melbourne (one in 416). The United States has more Whites than the entire population of Liverpool – an estimated total of just over 668,000 makes this their 15th most popular surname.

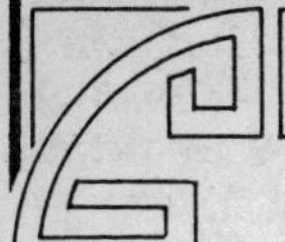

WILLIAMS

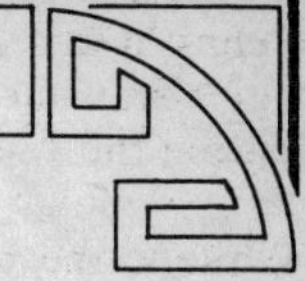

RELATED NAMES

Other surnames which are related as to root, derivation or usage include:

Fitzwilliam	Wilkie	Willett	Willmot
Gillam	Wilkin	Willetts	Willmoth
Gwilliam	Wilkins	Willey	Willmott
Wellman	Wilkinson	William	Willock
Wilcock	Wilks	Williamson	Willocks
Wilcocks	Willcock	Willie	Willot
Wilcockson	Willcocks	Willies	Wills
Wilcox	Willcox	Willis	Willy
Wilkerson	Willes	Willison	Wilman
Wilkes	Willet	Willmet	Wilmot
	Wilmott	See also Wilson	

The surname Williams sometimes means the same as Williamson, while it sometimes denotes other dependants – servants, daughters, wives, and so on. All come from the first name William. This name is of Old Germanic origin, coming originally from the name Willahelm. This is formed from the words 'wilja' meaning 'will' and 'helm' meaning 'protection'. Thus the name was probably first given as a kind of talisman of hoped-for traits.

As the Old German name spread, it became Normanised to Willelm. (In French it also became Guillaume, and as such gave rise to the English name Gillam). Compare Gaulter, Gautier for Walter, under Watson.

Following the Norman Conquest, William quickly became the most popular first name in the land, only being superseded by John in the middle of the twelfth century. Since then it has remained as one of our most popular first names, and has been the name of four kings. (Only Edward, Henry and George are more popular royal names.)

As one might expect, this popular first name gave rise to a number of diminutives and variations. Most of these have spawned their own variant surnames. Thus the diminutive Wylymot gives the surname Wilmot, and Willet and Willot arise similarly. The diminutive Wilkin gives Wilkins and Wilkinson, and the shortened form Will (for many years the most popular pet version, as in Will Shakespeare) gives us Wills and Wilson.

The name Williams is widespread throughout the land, but has special popularity in Wales. At the end of the last century one in every fourteen Welsh farmers was called Williams.

The earliest mention of Williams as a surname appears in the Domesday Book. Here in the records for 1086 one Robertus filius Willelmi is mentioned.

A WILLIAMS MISCELLANY

Ellen Cicely Wilkinson (1891–1947) was an English politician, labour organiser and suffragette who led the famous 1936 'Jarrow Crusade' as MP for the northern town of Jarrow, whose shipyard had been closed down in the Depression. Thousands of unemployed Geordies marched to London in a fruitless bid to obtain help from the government. Ellen Wilkinson died in office as Minister of Education, the first woman to hold that post.

*

One Williams has been Lord Mayor of London: Sir John Williams (1735).

*

William Carlos Williams (1883–1963) was one of America's greatest twentieth-century poets. In an era when Bohemian exile was the rule, Williams was an exception. As a home-town family doctor, his influential verse mirrored this practical streak and his love of everyday events.

*

Those great 'golden oldie' hits *Your Cheatin' Heart* and *Hey, Good Lookin'* were composed by the celebrated American country and western singer, Hank Williams (1923–53). Hank's style has played an influential role in much modern popular music.

*

The first fighting tank, manufactured by William Foster and Company of Lincoln, was nicknamed 'Big Willie'.

*

The United Kingdom has one town and one body of water related to this surname: Williamscot and Williams lake. Canada has 4 namesake towns while the United States has 24, including 5 called Williams. Australia also has a Williams as well as a Williamsburg. Geographic Williams's are fairly common, with rivers in Canada (2) and Australia as well as mountains in these two countries, while the Bahamas includes a Williams Island.

*

With about 451,000 namesakes Williams is the 3rd most popular surname in England and Wales. (The name is not common enough throughout Scotland to be counted separately.) Williams is notably popular in and around Cardiff where an estimated one in about 35 families bears the name. In decending numerical order Liverpool, Bristol and Birmingham are other Williams strongholds. Around the world Williams's are most common in Canberra (one in 232 families), Wellington (one in 237) and Sydney (one in 247). The United States has more Williams's than the entire population of Merseyside – an estimated total of just over 1,646,000 makes this their 3rd most popular surname.

WILSON

RELATED NAMES

Other surnames which are related as to root, derivation or usage include:

Fitzwilliam	Wilkes	Wilks	Willis
Gwilliam	Wilkie	Willcock	Willison
Wellman	Wilkin	Willet	Willmet
Wilcocks	Wilkins	Williamson	Willmot
Wilcox	Wilkinson	Willies	Willot

Wills Wilmot See also Williams

The name dates back to the ancient root word 'willahelm' which meant 'a willing man with a helmet' (i.e. protection). This word is largely intact today in the Germanic countries as Willem and Wilhelm. In Normandy it becomes Guillem. By the time of the Norman invasion of our country, this had become today's Guillaume. The name, along with Robert, Richard and John, was widely adopted in preference to Old English first names.

By the twelfth century derivations on William had become the most popular of all first names, accounting for fully 10 per cent of the entire male population registered on one of the rolls. Thus, early on, as efforts were made to distinguish one Will from another, the name was already destined to give rise to many of today's most popular surnames.

By 1324 we were getting close to today's name. That year's Court of Roles at the Manor of Wakefield in Yorkshire records a Robert Willeson. The first recorded Wilson per se was also in Yorkshire: Robert Wilson at Kirkstall in 1341.

Thereafter, during Henry IV's reign from the end of the fourteenth century onwards the '-son' ending was much in vogue. This was notably true in the north of the country.

Ever since, the fairly formal straightforward Wilson has predominated in the north, while in our southern counties less formal pet names gave rise to the diminutives Wilcocks and Wilkin, derived from the Dutch word 'ken' which means 'to know'.

The first record we have of the name in its formative stages is in the Domesday Book of 1086 which refers to a Robertus filius Willelmi (Robert son of William).

A WILSON MISCELLANY

'A week is a long time in politics' was a saying coined by Harold Wilson (b. 1916), one of Britain's longest-serving Prime Ministers. Earlier in his career he was the youngest Cabinet Minister since Pitt. Another great political Wilson was the American President, Woodrow Wilson (1856–1924). After the Allied victory in World War I, he master-minded the Versailles Peace Conference for which he was dubbed 'the architect of world peace'. During his last years in office he was a bed-ridden recluse and, unknown to the public, the affairs of state were virtually run by his wife.

*

Wilson's Disease is a hereditary condition leading to degeneration of the brain tissues.

*

Wilson's Promontory, the southernmost point on Australia's mainland, is named after Thomas Wilson, an English merchant. It boasts over 700 species of plants.

*

Eighteenth-century English mathematician John Wilson gave his name to Wilson's Theorem, the statement that sets criteria for what are natural prime numbers.

*

Sir Erasmus Wilson, early nineteenth-century surgeon and noted specialist on skin diseases, spent the vast wealth his practice brought him on charitable bequests and the promotion of Egyptian research. He paid £10,000 to have Cleopatra's Needle brought to London in 1878.

*

The United Kingdom has 3 towns which are related – 2 Wilsons and a Wilsontown. Canada has one, the curiously named Wilson's Prom, while the United States has 12 of which 9 are Wilsons. Australia has but one – Wilson Cliffs. Canada, the United States and Australia have Wilson lakes and rivers while the US has 3 Mount Wilsons including California's with its world-famed observatory. Australia also has a Wilson mountain.

*

With about 231,000 namesakes Wilson is the 11th most popular surname in England and Wales. There are over 46,000 Wilsons in Scotland where it is 3rd in popularity. In Ireland it is estimated that with about 14,000, Wilson is the 26th most popular surname. Wilson is notably popular in and around Edinburgh where an estimated one in about 95 families bears the name. In descending numerical order Glasgow, Teesside and Leeds are other Wilson strongholds. Around the world Wilsons are most common in Canberra (one in 230 families), Wellington (one in 237) and Auckland (one in 253). The United States has more Wilsons than the entire population of Leeds – an estimated total of just over 831,000 makes this their 10th most popular surname.

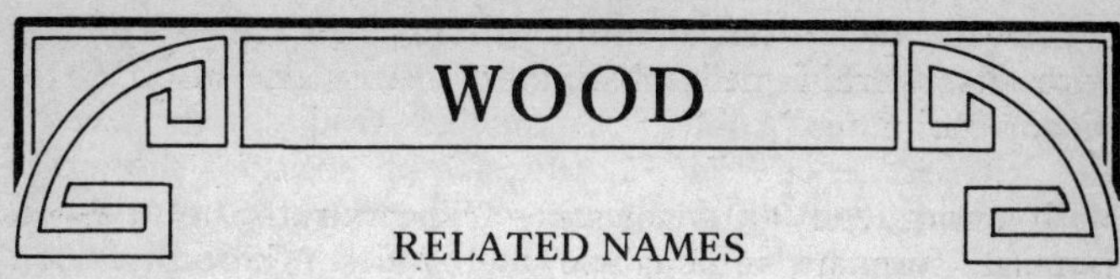

WOOD

RELATED NAMES

Other surnames which are related as to root, derivation or usage include:

Atwood	Woodard	Woodgrange	Woodman
Blackwood	Woodberry	Woodhall	Woodnutt
Boyce	Woodbine	Woodham	Woodroff
Dubois	Woodbridge	Woodhams	Woodroffe
Garwood	Woodburn	Woodhatch	Woodroof
Greenwood	Woodbury	Woodhead	Woodrow
Underwood	Woodcock	Woodhouse	Woodruff
Wode	Woodcraft	Woodhull	Woods
Wodehouse	Wooder	Wooding	Woodstock
Wodester	Woodeson	Woodland	Woodthorpe
Wodhams	Woodfield	Woodlay	Woodville
Woodall	Woodford	Woodley	Woodward

Wooster

Wood is one of many local surnames which derive from a particular geographical feature of a neighbourhood. Other common examples are Hill, Moore, Field, and so on. Until long after the Norman Conquest much of the English countryside was wooded, which accounts for the popularity of the name. An early usage of the name Wood (or Woods) comes in the form 'ate Wode', describing a person who lived 'at the wood'. To the Old English 'ate' was later added the definitive article in the dative form 'then' or 'ten', producing the Middle English 'atten'. This is retained in such names as Attenborough.

In the early years of the Norman Conquest surnames were given more as a form of description than as an actual name as we know it. Thus we find in the 1327 Subsidy Rolls for Somerset one William Wodeward, who was literally keeper or ward of the wood. However, by 1333 he was recorded merely as William in the Wode. Later still his descendants would become simply Wood.

One of the earliest mentions of the name Wood (in its original form) is in the 1273 Hundred Rolls for Oxford. Here there appear two Woods – Arthur ate Wode (at the wood) and Richard de la Wode. The French prepositions show the Norman influence on the language. The extreme Frenchified form still persists in the name Dubois (of the wood) which, despite its foreignness and popularity to this day across the Channel, is in England a name of extreme antiquity. On this side of the Channel the name dates from the centuries immediately following the Norman Conquest. By the thirteenth century these names were becoming increasingly anglicised, and the descendants of Richard de la Wode would almost certainly soon have become Richard ate Wode, and then either Attwood or plain Wood.

By the beginning of the fourteenth century Wood was prevalent as a family name all over England, and by then those with the name often had little to do with any actual woods. By this time Woods was a well-known family name except amongst the famous Surrey Woolmakers who operated from the woolmaking towns of Godalming, Wonersh and Farnham.

There are numerous surnames derived from the common root Wood, many of them from place names. These include not only the obvious Blackwood, Greenwood, Woodman and Woodward, but also several more obscure forms. Woodard, for instance, derives from wood-herd meaning a man who looked after animals in the woods. (In medieval times pigs were often grazed in woods.) However, not all similar Wood-related names derive from this common source. Some derive from Woader, meaning a dyer who used the dye woad (which the Ancient Britons used to paint themselves with before going into battle). Woad was a very popular blue dye made from a herb known in Anglo-Saxon as 'wād'. The name Wodester (from which we get the fine old Wodehousian name Wooster) also derives from this source. The name Wodehouse (or Woodhouse) meant a man who lived in a house in the woods (not a man who lived in a wooden house, since almost all houses were made of wood in those days). Yet Woodhouse was not a general name. It referred to certain distinct places, located chiefly in West Yorkshire, Derbyshire, Lincolnshire and Nottinghamshire. In rare cases, however, this name derived from the Old English word 'woodwose' which means 'a faun, satyr or troll', and often denoted a 'wild man'. (It is likely that the phrase 'a wild man of the woods' orginates from an early popular muddling of these words.)

There is also another similar rare derivation of the primary name Wood. In Old English the word 'wode' (or 'wood') also meant 'mad or frantic'. That is what Shakespeare means when he writes in *A Midsummer Night's Dream* of someone being 'wood within his wood'.

The earliest reference is to one Adam le Wode who appears in the 1221 Assize Rolls for Worcestershire.

A WOOD MISCELLANY

'Wood's half-pence' was named for William Wood, English ironmaster who purchased the right to coin half-pences and farthings for Ireland in 1722. His excessive profits led to a new Irish tax, prompting satirist Jonathan Swift's *Drapier's Letters* which spearheaded opposition and soon resulted in the patent being revoked.

*

The creator of the London 'Proms' was Sir Henry Wood (1867–1944). These promenade concerts, intended to bring classical music to a wider audience of young people, are an annual event, running nightly during the late summer, usually at the Albert Hall. These concerts started in 1897, and were conducted by Henry Wood every year from then on until his death.

*

The architecture of Georgian Bath is largely the work of John Wood (1704–54). His elegant Palladian designs for the Royal Crescent, Circus and parades were constructed in distinctive yellow Bath stone supplied by his patron, Ralph Allen.

*

The pay-as-you-earn income-tax scheme was devised by English statesman Sir Kingsley Wood.

*

British-born composer Haydn Wood is best remembered as composer of the popular song *Roses of Picardy*. He also wrote a string of music-hall hits, before concentrating on serious compositions after his Fantasy String Quartet won an important chamber-music prize.

*

As a geographic descriptive surname Woods are predictably thick on the ground. The United Kingdom alone has 122 place names which range from Wood Dalling to Woodyates and include such exotics as Woodside of Arbedie and Woodstock Slop. Canada has 17 Wood-related towns, while the United States has 63 including no fewer than 6 Woodstocks. South Africa and Australia each have 2, while New Zealand and Ireland each have 3, and Singapore has a Woodlands. Geographic named features are very common.

*

With about 172,000 namesakes Wood is the 22nd most popular surname in England and Wales. There are over 12,000 Woods in Scotland where it is 54th in popularity. Wood is notably popular in and around Bradford where an estimated one in about 155 families bears the name. In descending numerical order Leeds, Manchester and Sheffield are other Wood strongholds. Around the world Woods are most common in Sydney (one in 618 families), Auckland (one in 647) and Wellington (one in 723). The United States has more Woods than the entire population of Plymouth – an estimated total of just over 271,000 makes this their 62nd most popular surname.

WRIGHT

RELATED NAMES

Other surnames which are related as to root, derivation or usage include:

Arkwright	Sievewright	Wreight	Wrightson
Cartwright	Wheelwright	Wrickson	Wrigson
Cheesewright	Wraight	Wrighte	Wrixon
Faber	Wraighte	Wrightman	Wryght
Playwright	Wrate	Wrighton	Wrygson

Wrytte

The surname Wright is an occupational name from the Old English word 'wyrhta' which means 'a carpenter or joiner'. In early times almost everything was made of wood, and this occupational name covered a huge variety of trades. These we find in the comparatively rare compound surnames Wheelwright, Arkwright (box-maker), Cartwright and Sievewright. Later, the word 'wright' became synonymous with 'worker', and in many of the records this names is Latinised to Faber. (This also happened to many people called Smith, which see). As the meaning of 'wright' came to spread to all trades, many compounds were formed for skills which involved no connection with wood – amongst these are Playwright, and the lesser known Cheesewright (which remains as a rare surname).

The word 'wright' has long been in common usage in England. In literature, we find Chaucer using it in the fourteenth century. He mentions a man who 'was a well good wright, a carpenter'. However, the surname Wright appears even earlier.

Other common variations on the original name are Wrighte, Wraight(e), Wrate and Wreight.

One of the earliest references to the name is found in the Feet of Fines records for Sussex in 1214 where a Patere le Writh is mentioned.

A WRIGHT MISCELLANY

The Wright Brothers – Orville (1871–1948) and Wilbur (1867–1912) – have gone down in history as the designers of the first heavier-than-air flying machine. Their 745lb wheel-less biplane powered by a 12hp motor first took to the air on 17 December 1903 at Kill Devil Hill near Kitty Hawk, North Carolina. Airborne for 12 seconds, it travelled about 10 feet above the ground with Orville strapped into the driving seat, for 120 feet before taking a nose dive. Nicknamed Wright Flyer I, it now hangs in the Smithsonian Institution in Washington.

*

British physician Sir Almroth Wright was noted for his work in developing an anti-typhoid inoculation.

*

Two Wrights have been Lord Mayors of London: Edmund Wright in 1640 and Thomas Wright in 1785.

*

The United Kingdom has one related place name – Wrightington Bar, while Canada has 3 (one Wright and 2 Wrightsvilles) and the United States has 7 ranging from Wright to Wrightwood. Australia has a Wright lake; Canada has a Wright mountain; and the United States has a Wrightson mountain.

*

With about 194,000 namesakes Wright is the 13th most popular surname in England and Wales. There are over 10,000 Wrights in Scotland where it is 68th in popularity. Wright is notably popular in and around Nottingham where an estimated one in about 200 families bears the name. In descending numerical order Leicester, Sheffield and Leeds are other Wright strongholds. Around the world Wrights are most common in Sydney (one in 563 families), Auckland (one in 568) and Wellington (one in 584). The United States has more Wrights than the entire population of Bristol – an estimated total of just over 453,000 makes this their 29th most popular surname.

YOUNG

RELATED NAMES

Other surnames which are related as to root, derivation or usage include:

Yong	Youngblood	Younger	Youngman
Yonge	Younge	Younghusband	Youngmay
	Youngs	Youngson	

The surname Young derives from the Old English 'geong', meaning 'young', and from the Middle English word 'yong', or 'yung'. Initially this name could have been given as a nickname, either with reference to its bearer's appearance or, more usually, to distinguish the bearer from his father, who may well have had the same name. In this sense 'yung' would mean 'junior'. This is similar to the modern American use of the word junior (as in, for example, Kurt Vonnegut Jnr). Very occasionally the word is used to distinguish two brothers.

There are many variations on the surname Young. The most frequent of these are Youngs (son of Young), Younge, Yonge and Younger. A frequent compound variation is the name Younghusband. This is an occupational name and has nothing to do with marriage. Here 'husband' is used in the sense which remains in our word 'husbandry'. Thus Younghusband means 'young farmer'. Youngman is also an occupational name and means 'young servant', or simply 'servant'. To this day, this term is still used occasionally in London clubs to waiters (who are often far from young), and this sense remains in the French word for a waiter, which is 'garcon' meaning 'boy' or 'young man'. Another widespread variation is the predictable Youngson, whose meaning is self-evident. The variant Younger occasionally has a less obvious meaning. This is when the name derives from the Middle Dutch word 'jonghheer', which means 'young nobleman' (much like the similar German word 'Junker').

This name is one of the oldest to appear in the records, and references to it go back well before the Norman Conquest.

The earliest mention of a name stemming from this meaning is in the Anglo-Saxon Chronicle in the records for Essex. Here, in 744, one Wilferth seo Iunga is mentioned.

A YOUNG MISCELLANY

The Young–Helmholtz theory explains colour vision as resulting from separate retina fibres for red, green and blue light. The theory is named after Thomas Young (1773–1829) and, of course, Hermann Ludwig Ferdinand von Helmholtz (1821–94). Young also established the wave theory of light, and assisted in deciphering the Rosetta Stone.

*

Jazz great, Lester 'Pres' Young, got an early start: at the age of 10 he became a drummer in his father's New Orleans Show. Switching to the saxophone at 13, he made his name when he started playing with the legendary trumpeter, Joe 'King' Oliver, in Kansas City, later joining Count Basie's band for 10 years. His unique, sparse but buoyant sound triggered a bitter controversy which ranged through the jazz world for 15 years. Young's long-term love affair with Billie Holiday led to a series of recordings still regarded as masterpieces.

*

US astronaut John Young joined Virgil Grisson on the first two-man space flight, Gemini 3. Seventeen years later he orbited the moon on the final check-out of the Apollo systems before the successful Apollo 11 flight.

*

Sir Francis Younghusband (1863–1942), born in India, was a key member of the 1902 expedition which opened Tibet to the Western world. The main purpose of the expedition was to begin trade negotiations; when the first attempt was unsuccessful, the team undiplomatically slaughtered some 600 Tibetans, occupied the capital, Llasa, and forced the concession of a trade treaty on the Dalai Lama. A grateful England knighted Younghusband.

*

The United Kingdom has one related place name – Young's End, while Canada has 2 (Young and Youngstown) and the United States has 10 including 5 Youngsvilles. Australia has a town called Young, and so does Uruguay. The name is common for geographic features and sometimes refers to the geologic age of the mountain or body of water so named.

*

With about 105,000 namesakes Young is the 50th most popular surname in England and Wales. There are over 21,000 Youngs in Scotland where it is 19th in popularity. Young is notably popular in and around Edinburgh where an estimated one in about 185 families bears the name. In descending numerical order, Glasgow, Bristol and Teesside are other Young strongholds. Around the world Youngs are most common in Wellington (one in 361 families), Toronto (one in 509) and Auckland (one in 515). The United States has more Youngs than the entire populations of Southampton and Portsmouth combined – an estimated total of just over 478,000 makes this their 26th most popular surname.

SURNAME INDEX

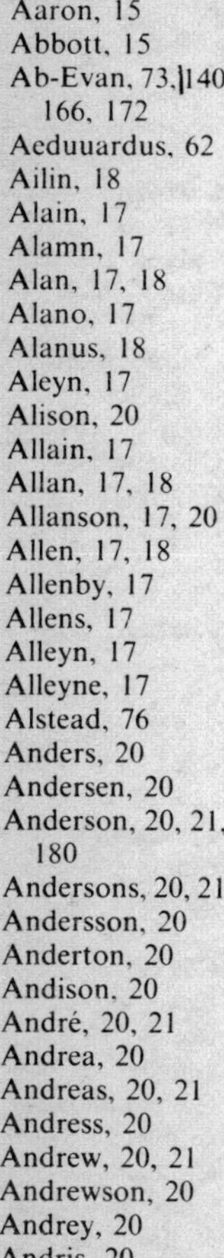

SURNAME INDEX

SURNAME INDEX

SURNAME INDEX

SURNAME INDEX

SURNAME INDEX

SURNAME INDEX

SURNAME INDEX